"Queen of the Bootleggers"
By Kirk McCracken

QUEEN OF THE BOOTLEGGERS

Chapter 01   Queen of the Bootleggers
Chapter 02   A Business Meeting
Chapter 03   Cleo Epps
Chapter 04   Stomping Grounds
Chapter 05   Nelson's Car Bombing
Chapter 06   Bootlegging
Chapter 07   Lost and Found
Chapter 08   Crime and the depression
Chapter 09   McDonald and Pugh
Chapter 10   Three Witness, Three Murders
Chapter 11   The Dixie Mafia
Chapter 12   Bombs, Bombs & More Bombs
Chapter 13   The Murder Trial of Cleo Epps
Chapter 14   A Final Legacy

CHAPTER ONE
Queen of the Bootleggers

Anyone walking by her final resting place would think 61-year old Cleo Epps lived a simple life. Her grave marker isn't elaborate. The 1-foot by 2-foot bronze plaque sits atop a white and grey marble slab that is just slightly bigger than the plaque. The bronze rectangular plate is adorned with embossed roses on each side with a small bronze flower vase at the top. The headstone simply has her name and years of life, "Cleo Epps 1909-1970."

What happened between 1909 and 1970 wasn't so simple. Cleo Epps was one of the biggest bootleggers in the Tulsa-Creek County area, living a life full of crime, whiskey, bootlegging, car bombings, murder, and the attempted murder of a district judge, all while caring for others with a heart of gold.

She wasn't necessarily involved in all of those situations, but she was affiliated with the unbelievable cast of characters that were involved. She had both direct, and indirect, links to these crimes, and her reputation either flourished or suffered depending on who is telling the story. However, one thing that isn't disputed is her love for others and a heart to help those in need.

Most bootleggers were either loved or hated. Epps was loved by nearly everyone, including police officers, lawyers, judges, and especially those in need of alcohol.

The grave marker also doesn't tell the tale of her bloody ending by the hands of a man she seemed to love at one point in her life.

In 1970, Cleo Epps died at the age of 61 years old but witnessed more in those years than most people do that live to be 100. Epps was considered a crime boss, specializing in illegal whiskey. She was in total control of several eastern Oklahoma counties, in the 1940s and 1950s, and was linked to several members of the "Dixie Mafia," a loosely-based not-so organized crime syndicate that committed crimes in Oklahoma and every state that surrounded it, and some that didn't.

Epps was a contradiction, to say the least.

She was warm and kind to others, and as a schoolteacher earlier in life, her fellow teachers and students thought of her as more of a mother-figure than a teacher or co-worker. She wanted to take care of people, especially children. She could also be big and brassy as a bootlegger. And, she was a crime boss no matter how you slice it, and crime bosses do whatever it takes to stay out of prison.

The number of times Epps was married is disputed within her family. Several family members have different versions of how many times she tied the knot. The most popular version is that Epps was married four times to three different men, and illegal whiskey seemed to be a big part of those marriages.

And, she might have been married a fifth time.

Her nickname, "The Bootleg Queen" or "Queen of the Bootleggers" was given to her by Tulsa Tribune reporter Nolen Bulloch in the 1940s, who wrote story after story in the prohibition era, painting a picture of the unbelievable characters for his readers.

She hated the nickname.

Epps would go out of her way to provide for people that were down on their luck, which included giving loans or gifts to make sure children had things like food, clothing, and shelter. She was also linked to men that committed numerous murders that took fathers away from their children.

She was a contradiction.

Epps did not condone these acts, but she was associated with the men that carried them out. She even helped hide and care for criminals that were on the run from the law.

There were two versions of Cleo Epps.

One version was that of a hard-working, tough-as-nails businesswoman that could be seen on the roof of a house hanging shingles while wearing work boots and work clothes. She would also dress this way while hauling cases of whiskey from Missouri and Arkansas in one of her work trucks, semi-trailers or dump trucks.

On the days she was building houses or painting barns on her property, she chose work clothes and boots over dresses and dress shoes. Her clothes were often covered in dirt and grime, accented with paint splatter from the hard work she put in that day.

Epps didn't look like a normal 60-plus year-old grandmother. She wasn't obsessed with her looks, and she wasn't sporting gray hair that was shaped perfectly round underneath a scarf. She didn't have cheap black horn-rimmed glasses with the fancy chain/necklace that held them in place. She didn't wear old dresses with pantyhose rolled below the knee and comfortable heels.

The second version was that of a beautiful woman dressed to the nines in the latest fashions with nice high-heel shoes, gorgeous jewelry, and a hairstyle that matched. When she was entertaining company or out running errands, Epps looked immaculate, and she could turn the heads of both men and women. Men were attracted to her, and women were jealous of her clothes and accessories.

Epps didn't really look like she belonged in the illegal whiskey business, but she had no trouble maneuvering in that world. She was a slightly-older-than-middle-aged white woman with black hair and a warm and inviting smile. She wasn't skinny, but she wasn't fat. Epps was strong, muscular, and could do the work of any man. Her fingernails often had dirt under them because she chose to do the work on her land rather than pay someone to do it for her.

Epps was in total control of everything she did.

She could handle herself in any situation, and she was afraid of no man. However, she knew too much and trusted the wrong people.

Epps partnered with underworld criminals like Thomas Lester Pugh, Albert "Big Al" McDonald, and

Kirksey Nix Jr. who were associates in the Dixie Mafia. They dealt mainly in theft, robberies, arson-for-hire, and the occasional murder. However, in the latter 1960s and early 1970s, bombings were all the rage for criminal organizations. A lot of bad people, and good people, wound up on the receiving end of a few sticks of dynamite.

Albert McDonald was a tall white man, standing at around 6-foot-2. He had jet-black wavy hair that was sometimes curly. He was a strong man that had a slight belly, and he was mean. He was mean and didn't try to pretend not to be.

Lester Pugh was nearly a direct contrast to McDonald. He was short at about 5-foot-6 with straight blondish-brown hair, parted to the side. Pugh often put on the persona of being a nice and loveable guy, but he could turn around and kill the person to which he was showing affection. The criminal team of McDonald and Pugh was deadly. They were killers, plain and simple. They stole anything that wasn't tied down, and they had no remorse for any of the crimes they committed, and they rarely admitted guilt.

Epps wasn't afraid to get her hands dirty in the illegal whiskey business and made runs all of the time, driving to different states to either deliver or pick up truckloads of hooch. She mainly drove to Missouri and Arkansas, bought the whiskey, and drove it back to Oklahoma.

She once said, "When I invest $10,000 in a load of whiskey, I'll be doing the driving myself."

Despite being well-respected, liked, and adored, she committed the only unforgivable sin in the criminal underworld.

Cleo Epps, the queen of the bootleggers, was a rat.

CHAPTER TWO
A Business Meeting

"I'll be right there. Just gimme a second," Cleo Epps said in almost a low whisper as she walked away from Albert McDonald.

Epps was having dinner with friends, John and Loda Bough, at the Bough's house, which was located on Epps' property. Through her lucrative business practices over the years, Epps was able to purchase property all over the area and owned numerous rent houses, tons of land, and a few motels.

It was around 6 p.m. and it was starting to get dark, but it was still light outside.

The Boughs weren't just friends. They were like family. They were living in one of the houses Epps built and owned, and she had dinner with them almost every night. This night was no different.

John Bough and Epps were exhausted from painting a barn and several rent houses on her property, and they both had spots of paint on their clothes and shoes. Epps still had on the green slacks and white sweater she was wearing while painting all day. The three were trying to unwind after a long day.

Epps looked at the Boughs as she was getting ready to leave with McDonald and said, "I'll be right back."

McDonald was there on business. It wasn't out of the ordinary, but business dealings involving whiskey were fewer and further between now in 1970 than they were during prohibition over 10 years earlier. Epps had all but gotten out of the bootlegging business, but she still had a few money-making ventures that never went away just because whiskey became legal. She had a few customers that bought whiskey for a fair price, and they didn't have to pay taxes to the government for it.

Generally, business calls weren't a matter of concern, but now, Epps was cautious. Over the past month or so, Epps was constantly looking over her shoulder.

Epps didn't even put on a coat. She grabbed her truck keys and walked out of the front door and onto the porch, and McDonald was waiting for her. He told Epps to meet him and his partner Lester Pugh at the Union Square Shopping Center, located at 51st and Union Avenue in West Tulsa. It wasn't very far from her property, which was located four miles northeast of Sapulpa, Oklahoma. Pugh and McDonald drove away from the Bough's house in a 1970 dark-colored four-door Dodge sedan.

It was Thursday, November 12, 1970 in Tulsa, Oklahoma, and the temperature was a brisk 35-degrees. It was windy, cloudy and cold. The sun had already disappeared from the sky for the day, refusing to provide any warmth to the 61-year old semi-retired bootlegger.

Epps walked outside to her old pearlized green and white colored pickup truck. She slid onto the cold leather seat and shivered as she started the engine, waiting for the truck to warm-up. It was cold enough for her to see her breath, and the windshield had fogged up and had to be wiped down.

Mother Nature is quite bipolar in Oklahoma. In November it could be warm, sunny and 70-degrees or bitter cold and near below zero with ice and snow, and those two vastly different temperatures could happen in the span of 24 hours.

On February 10, 2011, in Nowata, Oklahoma, the temperature was recorded at (-31) degrees, the lowest temperature ever in the state of Oklahoma. A week later, it was 79-degrees and sunny. The temperature rose 110-degrees in only a week.

The Boughs saw Epps pull away from their house, and it was the last time they would see Epps alive.

She had to make one more stop. If Epps had a best friend it was Billie Popovich, and Epps needed to stop by her house to talk about McDonald's surprise visit. Popovich lived near the Avalon Steakhouse, and it was on the way to the meeting place down Union Avenue. It was basically a straight shot from Popovich's house. Before the two were able to discuss much, Epps received two phone calls from McDonald. He knew where she was, and he was growing impatient.

Epps stopped by Popovich's house to get encouragement from a friend. Epps knew her days were numbered for several different reasons.

Popovich also watched Epps leave, and she never saw her friend again.

Epps was headed to West Tulsa for a private meeting with business associates McDonald and Pugh, but they weren't just business associates. They were also friends, and McDonald was a bit more than that to Epps. She once considered marrying McDonald, who was around 15 years her junior at 45 years old, and he would have been her fourth, fifth or sixth husband, depending on who you ask. They were seen together so much that everyone thought they were going to be married, but McDonald started dating the widow of a Bartlesville, Oklahoma man who was a fence for stolen jewelry before his death. McDonald married the widow after a brief courtship.

A fence is someone who buys stolen merchandise and sells it for profit. They are the middleman between thieves and the eventual buyer.

The marriage of McDonald and the widow never sat well with Epps, but she maintained a working relationship with him.

While on the Bough's porch, just minutes earlier, Pugh and McDonald, two Dixie Mafia operatives, told Epps they needed to talk to her about a truckload of stolen whiskey they obtained. They needed to stash the stolen booze, and Epps had a lot of land with barns and houses that were being built. They could even bury the whiskey on her land in a pinch. The two needed her help, and she didn't have a choice. She had to go meet with them.

Epps knew that the two men weren't to be trusted, but she did, regardless. If she didn't meet them, it would be obvious. The queen of the bootleggers was a police informant and testified to a grand jury against Pugh and

McDonald about their involvement in a very high-profile case that occurred only a month prior. The grand jury proceeding was sealed, and the witnesses were supposed to be a mystery.

She knew if she fled the state or did anything out of the ordinary, she would confirm any suspicion the two criminals might have about her. She couldn't look, talk, or act any different outside of her normal behavior.

During the September hearing, Epps testified against the two men while in disguise, and her name was sealed, but for the right price, anyone could find out who testified in closed proceedings in Tulsa, Oklahoma, at the time. She didn't know for sure if Pugh and McDonald knew about her testimony against them but trying to kill a sitting district judge carried a heavy prison sentence, and Epps' testimony could bury them.

If she didn't testify against them, it could bury her with the law. She had a prior bootlegging conviction hanging over her head that was being appealed and there really wasn't a right decision. She was damned either way.

Around three months earlier in August 1970, Tulsa County District Judge Fred S. Nelson was critically injured in a car bombing outside of his home, and the bombing is believed to be politically motivated. Pugh and McDonald reportedly wanted Judge Nelson off of the bench to make way for a more sympathetic judge. The Dixie Mafia needed Judge Nelson, a republican, out of commission or dead in order for his opponent, democratic candidate Charles Pope, to win the judicial seat in the general election.

Epps knew the two men were behind the explosion and testified against McDonald and Pugh in a closed grand jury proceeding that took place on Monday, September 28, 1970, in the Tulsa County Courthouse with District Attorney S.M. Buddy Fallis representing the state.

Grand jury proceedings are secret, and the witnesses, the grand jury, and the prosecution take an oath not to divulge anything they learn during the hearing. Fallis kept the proceedings closed so he could eventually issue subpoenas for Pugh and McDonald, but word got out and the two ex-cons left town for a while.

During the proceedings, Epps, Arlis Delbert (A.D.) Self, and Georgia Whipple Jenkins, the wife of criminal Bob Jenkins, testified against Pugh and McDonald. The grand jury adjourned five days later on Friday, October 2, 1970, and the jury returned no indictments. The investigation continued. The state needed more evidence.

Dynamite was used in the car bombing of Judge Nelson, and it was Epps' dynamite. Before the assassination attempt, a neighbor saw Epps and McDonald talking on her West Tulsa property. The conversation was private, and she couldn't hear what either Epps or McDonald were saying. However, the man was animated and kept pointing to a hole in the ground. Epps crossed her arms and walked away, and McDonald reached down into the hole and picked up several items before leaving.

The neighbor couldn't see what he retrieved from the hole, but McDonald wasn't really trying to conceal what he was carrying back to his car either. McDonald did whatever McDonald wanted to do.

He knew Epps used dynamite for breaking up stumps on her land, and he knew where she kept it.

A day after the bombing, Jack McKenzie, an investigator for Creek and Okfuskee Counties drove his car to Epps' house and observed Epps, Pugh, and McDonald talking in front of her house. Later that day, McKenzie called Epps and the two talked for a while. McKenzie and Epps were close and had established a friendship along with their working relationship as policeman and police informant.

Epps told the investigator that McDonald and Pugh wanted the dynamite, and she was afraid of what they might do with it. McKenzie then returned to the Epps house after their phone conversation and went straight to the hole or "pond bank" in the yard. He dug in that same spot with his hands and quickly found a steel box that contained more sticks of dynamite.

Epps told McKenzie that McDonald said he needed the dynamite for a "union job," but she didn't believe him.

The day after the bombing, Epps spoke with McKenzie and she was visibly upset and crying about the car bombing. She was haunted about what could have happened.

She told McKenzie, "I never dreamed they'd do something like that. What if that little (Nelson) girl had gotten into the car with her daddy?"

If Epps wanted to avoid prison for the attempted murder of a government official she had to testify against her associates, Pugh and McDonald, and District Attorney S.M. Buddy Fallis convinced her it was the only way. She had to testify.

That's exactly what she did on September 28, 1970 to the grand jury. However, Epps was known in the Tulsa area by criminals, police officers, judges, lawyers, and city officials, and the one place that has all of them is the Tulsa County Courthouse. She couldn't take the chance of being seen and went to great lengths to conceal her identity. That Monday morning, Epps walked into the Tulsa Courthouse, wearing a red wig, dark horn-rimmed sunglasses, and a long coat to hide the shape of her body. Epps was now dressed more like a grandmother. She walked right passed District Attorney Fallis, who knew her very well, and he did not recognize her.

Fallis said in all of his years in the district attorney's office, he had never seen a witness resort to such great lengths to not be identified. However, she wasn't the only one afraid of the Dixie Mafia. Fellow witness, A.D. Self, hid in the judge's chambers until it was his time to testify, attempting to avoid anyone that might recognize him.

A grand jury proceeding is used by the prosecution to get an indictment against a suspect. The cases are generally serious felonies, and the prosecution presents the case to the grand jury, and they decided if an indictment should be brought against the suspect, making him a defendant.

Some grand jury members are called for jury duty for months at a time but only appear a few days out of the month. Neither guilt nor innocence is decided during grand jury proceedings, just whether or not there is enough evidence to indict a suspect.

The proceedings are more relaxed than a normal trial or preliminary hearing. There is no judge, and generally, there are no lawyers other than the prosecution. There are also fewer rules in regard to the introduction of evidence and testimony. The proceedings are not open to the public which encourages witnesses to testify openly and without fear, and it protects their identities in case there is no indictment or "true bill."

If an indictment is not handed down, a prosecutor can still take a suspect to trial, but it's harder to get a conviction. A grand jury proceeding is almost like a trial run to see if a prosecutor can convince a group of strangers that the suspect is guilty.

If an indictment is handed down, the trial generally starts sooner and fewer preliminary hearings are needed.

During her testimony, Epps was very polite, calm and gracious. She wasn't hostile or belligerent like some witnesses can be, especially witnesses that have a checkered past. And Epps had a checkered past.

The female bootlegger testified that Pugh and McDonald came to her property to take the dynamite used in the car bomb for Judge Nelson.

But now, it's a cold November night, the grand jury hearing was over a month old, and Epps was meeting her business partners in a shopping center parking lot. Epps pulled her truck into a parking space next to Pugh and McDonald who had been waiting for her. McDonald was driving and Pugh was in the backseat. Epps got out of her truck and walked toward the four-door car. McDonald waved and pointed to the empty front passenger seat.

Epps opened the door and sat down in the front seat next to McDonald, who immediately pulled out of the parking lot and drove south down Union Avenue. They crossed the bridge over Interstate 44 and headed towards an area with only a few housing additions scattered about and plenty of farmland. There was a lot of open land.

McDonald was doing all of the talking, but Epps wasn't really paying attention. Something didn't feel right, but her mind could be playing tricks on her. They've had odd meetings before, and she convinced herself to relax just a little bit.

In the backseat, directly behind Epps, Pugh was quiet. He slowly grabbed a white towel from the floorboard, raised his pant leg, and pulled a .22 caliber pistol from his boot. The towel was to keep blood from getting all over the car, and the gun was for revenge.

McDonald pulled the car over, parking on a piece of land near a pasture where horses were grazing. He pretended he needed to stop the car so he could have a more in-depth conversation with Epps.

From the backseat, Pugh raised the towel and the gun to the back of Epps' head and pulled the trigger. With the windows rolled up, the loud bang and bright flash of light were amplified inside the car, which was now filled with smoke and the smell of gunpowder. The towel didn't stop the blood spatter. Epps's body sunk down in her seat, and her head fell to the side. The towel didn't do its job, and blood was splattered on the passenger side door.

Pugh then wrapped her head in the towel and placed a rubber band around it to keep it in place. The towel was now used to soak up any blood that flowed from the bullet wound in Epps' head.

McDonald put the car in drive and pulled back out onto Union Avenue. They headed south again towards 71st street, stopping near 65th and Union where they were going to dispose of the body, but, like the towel, the gun hadn't done its job either.

They were now in front of three abandoned adobe-style rock and wood houses, located just off of Union Avenue. In about seven years, Page Belcher Golf Course would open directly across the street.

McDonald got out of the car and opened the passenger door, which moved Epps' body.

Epps, loudly inhaled, taking a deep breath of cold winter air. She sat up in her seat and tried to look around, attempting to get her bearings. Blood was pouring from a bullet wound in the back of her head, and her face was covered with the towel, preventing her from seeing anything around her. She turned towards the backseat, then to the driver's side and then to the open door that was letting in the cold air.

Epps then exclaimed, "Lester, you killed me. You didn't have to do that."

Pugh calmly raised the gun again and shot her in the head a second time.

The queen of the bootleggers was now dead.

CHAPTER THREE
Cleo Epps

Cleo (Gilbert) Epps was born September 26, 1909 in Magazine, Arkansas, a small city located in Logan County. Less than 50 miles from the Oklahoma border, Magazine has never had more than 1,000 residents living in the town, and according to the 1910 census, there were 968 residents around the time Epps was born, which is the most in the town's history.

She was born to parents Richard Mosley Gilbert Jr. and Sarah Daisy (Groh) Gilbert, and they had two sons, as well. Samuel Clifford Gilbert was born in 1908, a year before Cleo, and Thomas Richard Gilbert was born four years after her in 1913.

Logan County was formed on March 22, 1871, but it was originally named Sarber County after J. Newton Sarber, a senator from the Sixth District. The county was pieced together from parts of Franklin, Scott, Johnson, and Yell counties, and the landscape consists of rolling farmlands, forested ridges, mountains, and several lakes. The county can also lay claim to the highest point in Arkansas, Mt. Magazine, which is 2,753-feet high.

Four years later, on December 14, 1875, the legislature voted to change the name from Sarber to Logan County after Colonel James Logan, a pioneer in that part of Arkansas.

Logan County houses parts of two national forests, the Ozark National Forest and the Ouachita National

Forest, where people come from all over the world to camp, hike, swim, and fish.

Paris, Arkansas is Logan's county seat.

Established just after the Civil War, the town of Magazine, Arkansas was given its name from the tallest Mountain in the state, Mt. Magazine. Located less than 10 miles from the mountain, Magazine sits close to State Highways 10 and 109, but it was established well before the highways were built.

In 1867, an Illinois businessman and merchant, Eli D. Hooper, moved to Arkansas and, three years later, established a store where Magazine sits today. By 1883, Magazine had several stores and was on its way to becoming a metropolis with over 200 residents and a Methodist Church.

By the early 1890s, Magazine had doubled its residents and established several churches, a cotton gin, had a handful of doctors, more than one drug store, two blacksmith shops, a school, and a grist mill.

In 1899, a storm caused severe damage to the town, but the citizens banded together and immediately started rebuilding.

After the turn of the century, the Magazine Gazette Newspaper was established, and the town became a place of work and leisure, but it also successfully produced and exported peaches, hay, clover, cotton, and corn.

The timber industry reached its peak by 1910, and, in the 1920s, crop disease, and unpredictable and severe weather hammered orchard farms. Cotton prices bottomed out after World War I, and a drought in the early 1930s devastated the region. Too many farmers were trying to work on too many farms through sharecropping, and the weather and failed crops led to a depression.

Cleo Epps moved to Oklahoma from Arkansas in the 1920s. Her family claims she graduated high school at age 16 and attended Northeastern State Teachers College, earning a teaching degree at age 18. She reportedly earned a college education in a time when dropping out of high school around the eighth grade was more likely.

However, Northeastern State University has no record of Epps every attending college there.

She started her professional career as a schoolteacher and taught in Oklahoma's Wagoner and Creek Counties.

She first taught at Stoney Point, an elementary school in Wagoner County, near Yonkers, Oklahoma, and neither the school nor the town exist anymore, for the most part. The area was flooded to make Ft. Gibson Lake, and Stoney Point is now under water. There is an area that is said to be Yonkers, but it is considered a ghost town and only a few concrete slabs from homes and businesses still exist.

Technically, there are a few houses in the area.

After leaving the Wagoner area, Epps moved to Creek County.

In West Tulsa, near the town of Sapulpa, Epps taught at Bowden School. Bowden was a small community about the size of a neighborhood, but the

Bowden school doesn't exist anymore. Bowden merged with the Allen school that was near Bowden, and now, Allen-Bowden School is a pre-K through eighth-grade school with around 300 students.

Bowden School was Epps' last teaching job before she got into the full-time illegal whiskey trade. She also taught at Rock Creek and Pleasant Valley Schools in Creek County.

Her father, Richard Mosley Gilbert, Jr., died at age 54 on August 25, 1933 and is buried in Bethel Cemetery, in Magazine, Arkansas. His grave marker is a cement rectangle, the size of a brick that reads: "R.M.J.R. GILBERT" with a drawn heart. The name and heart were drawn on the brick while the cement was still wet.

Illegal whiskey just seemed to be a part of Epps's adult life. In her several marriages, booze was a prominent theme.

According to her family, Epps was married four times, twice to the same man, Cecil Epps, a bootlegger.

Cleo Epps and Cecil Epps had their marriage annulled after only a few days when her father found out. Actually, her father had the marriage annulled, and Cleo Epps started learning about the bootlegging business around that same time.

She married a second time to Miles "Jack" Joice after she moved to Oklahoma. After her second marriage lasted less than a year, she married her third husband, a Tulsa lawyer, but he drank too much.

It is rumored that during one of her marriages she gave birth to a son that died as an infant, and she battled and beat ovarian cancer as a young woman. Due to the cancer, she couldn't have children.

After her third marriage failed, Epps married Cecil Epps again, but by then, she had her own operation. Her fourth marriage to, what was her first husband, didn't last very long, and they divorced... again.

Some say she only married Cecil Epps once, but she did marry him at least once.

Epps also testified during a trial after her fourth marriage that she was briefly married to a man with the last name Clawthorne. She might have been married a fifth time but said Clawthorne died the day before her final arrest in 1966.

Her first, and maybe fourth husband, Cecil Epps, was a bootlegger, but he wasn't a very good bootlegger. He was a bootlegger that drank too much, which is a problem.

Cleo Epps was now in charge of the biggest bootleg operation in the area, and she didn't need a man to help her. She was also a fence for stolen items, including cars.

Epps was attracted to "bad boys" and that was evident by her choice of husbands and boyfriends. According to her family, none of her husbands were "any good," and a former boyfriend was responsible for her untimely death.

Epps dealt in truckloads of illegal booze and made a lot of money doing so. She once said, "I never sold a bottle of whiskey in my life. All I did was drive it across the state line. Everybody knows that."

Cecil Epps was a good teacher, in a way. He showed Cleo Epps his way of being a bootlegger. She did the exact opposite, and it made her successful.

She was always strictly against whiskey and never drank the stuff. However, whiskey made bootleggers truckloads of money, and she eventually said, "To hell with it" and started her journey in the seedy world of whiskey running and criminal enterprise.

Epps took over Cecil's business because he was often too drunk to make deliveries, making it her responsibility to keep his less-than-legal obligations. She saw how much money could be made and ended her career as a teacher to deliver whiskey full-time.

Early in her illegal whiskey operation, Epps was hauling a truckload of whiskey from Missouri to Oklahoma, and she had a minor traffic accident inside the Missouri border. The police were called, the accident was quickly cleaned up, and Epps was sent on her way. However, Missouri officers called Oklahoma and warned them of Epp's illegal cargo.

To Epps, something seemed off, and she stashed the whiskey in the woods and drove across the border to Oklahoma where she was immediately pulled over by the police.

When officers searched her truck, they found nothing. She had several secret compartments on her truck, and officers looked in every one of them, but there was no whiskey.

"Alright, Mrs. Cleo, where's the booze?" an officer asked.

"I drank it," Epps said with a slight smile on her face.

Everyone knew Epps never drank alcohol, and the officers had to let her go.

Bootleggers couldn't just drive around with cases of whiskey in a flat-bed truck covered with a canvas tarp like in the movies. They had to get creative, and Epps would haul lumber with parts of the wood hollowed out to stash the cases of whiskey. Epps even had a semi-truck and a dump truck that she used to deliver large amounts of product.

She caught her first bootlegging charge and conviction in 1941. Then, other charges and convictions followed in 1942 and 1952. She pled guilty to the charges because she said she was guilty. She wasn't afraid to face the music.

She caught another bootlegging charge in 1955, and she was sentenced to jail for the third time in her life. Epps was sentenced to six months in jail and a $500 fine on the liquor importation charge but expected to get a much lesser sentence.

Epps testified against several men in a separate bootlegging conspiracy charge -- R.J. "Bob" Matthews, of Sioux City, Iowa, Benny Stewart, a Creek County nightclub operator, Melvin Hammatt, formerly of Sapulpa, and Tony Morris, of Chicago -- and the men eventually pleaded guilty to the charges. However, despite her testimony, Epps was given the same sentence as her 1952 conviction, six months in jail and a $500 fine.

Epps thought her testimony would grant her favor with the judge.

The Matthews-Stewart conspiracy involved the importation of 2,000 cases of liquor into Oklahoma every week, and they planned to take over the whiskey business in the state. Hammett, who was basically just a driver, was not a major conspirator.

On Tuesday, March 1, 1955, Epps walked out of the Federal Building in Tulsa, visibly shaken and in tears. In the past, Epps had taken her brushes with the law in an almost light-hearted manner, but this sentence was a shock, and she couldn't hide her emotions.

The Queen of the Bootleggers was going to jail for the third time in almost 15 years, but more importantly, this shows that Epps was a police informant long before her testimony to the 1970 grand jury.

The Matthews-Stewart conspiracy case was separate from her 1955 charge, and her attorneys asked that her sentencing be postponed until the disposition of the Matthews-Stewart case. But U.S. District Court Judge Royce H. Savage denied the motion and sentenced Epps. He also cited her previous 1952 sentence, which was from a similar charge.

The maximum sentence that could have been imposed was one year in jail and a $1,000 fine.

Her criminal record was read in court and it showed five offenses with two previous stints in jail, including an 11-month sentence that was served at the federal reformatory for women in Alderson, West Virginia.

She started serving her sentence in 1955, and it wasn't without controversy. Cleo Epps was accused of "running the jail" and "buying her way through" while she was serving her time in the federal part of the Tulsa County jail.

Halfway into her six-month sentence, a recently-released inmate named Victoria Roberts wrote a letter of complaint to James Bennett, the Director of the Bureau or Federal Prisons in Washington D.C. She also mailed a letter to the Tulsa Tribune.

Roberts, a black woman from Tulsa, claims Epps was given the run of the Tulsa County Jail and permitted by jail authorities to buy her way through on easy street, receiving all the comforts available, and some that weren't available.

Tulsa County Sheriff Glenn Brown denied all accusations and said that Epps was a trusty for the jail, which can give her certain privileges others might not get. Epps was a trustee in the records office and had limited access to other prisoner's records.

Roberts claimed Epp's privileges far exceeded those of a regular trustee.

Roberts, who was also serving time for a liquor charge, told the Tribune that Epps could be seen eating fried chicken dinners while other inmates ate what the jail provided, and Epps would wear normal clothing complete with jewelry while other inmates wore county-issued clothing.

She even claims Epps could be seen carrying keys to the jail at any given time.

The Tribune was told that bail bondsman E.C. "Red" Carter brought the chicken dinners to Epps, but he denied the accusation. However, Carter said he knew who did bring the special dinners to Epps but refused to reveal the person's identity.

In Roberts' letter, she wrote: "I was found guilty of committing a federal offense and sentenced to six months confinement in the Tulsa County jail of the federal prisons. I was admitted February 11 and released on July 10. As a result of serving my time as a federal prisoner in the Tulsa County jail, I have these grievances to make:

"1. There was a great deal of partiality shown by the matron toward some prisoners. I was not given any favorable treatment whatsoever but, in my estimation, and opinion, I was grossly mistreated along with other Negro female prisoners.

"I found that the white girls, especially those with financial backing, were allowed to wear their diamond rings, their everyday clothing with shoes to match and on several occasions, were fed a different kind of food than we as colored persons.

"There was one federal prisoner, Mrs. Cleo Epps, who was given greater privileges than all others. She was admitted March 16, received a trustee appointment, given a private room, given access to personal files of other prisoners, allowed to make phone calls as freely as she desired, and served very little time in a cell behind bars.

"The matron, Mrs. Estelle Guise, did not extend such privileges to other prisoners. I sincerely feel that Cleo Epps as a prisoner was permitted by the jail authorities to buy her way through on easy street and received all of the comforts available.

"I was told by Mrs. Scott, the probation officer, that one prisoner is no better than another, and if this is true, I feel as though there needs to be an investigation made of the Tulsa County jail and its confinement of federal prisoners."

Roberts also complained about the cleanliness of the jail and said the shower was out of order for the majority of her sentence. She also claimed the matron, Mrs. Guise, would punish the black female prisoner more harshly than the white prisoners.

She ended with: "I sincerely hope that you will see fit to investigate my complaints and that something will be done to eliminate that partiality shown among prisoners and to ensure the equal treatment of all prisoners regardless as to their race, color, creed or financial status."

Again, Sheriff Glenn Brown denied the allegations saying: "there is not a thread of truth" in the letter. Brown also said that Roberts was "one of the worst troublemakers we have ever had. She wanted to run the jail and have special privileges. We have to run the jail."

Brown claims Roberts was always causing trouble and encouraged other prisoners to join her. She reportedly ripped up mattresses and used the stuffing to clog toilets.

The Tulsa World then published a story on Friday, July 29, 1955, where Sheriff Brown accuses Tribune writer Nolen Bulloch of not doing his research in regard to Roberts' letter.

Sheriff Brown accused Bulloch of "deliberately printing a malicious story with no attempt to find out the truth" and said the reporter "went out of his way to avoid learning the facts."

According to Brown, Epps asked for some work to do to pass the time while serving her sentence, and she was given a job as a trustee in the records room with two other prisoners.

Epps did not receive any credit for working in the records room. At the regular county jail, not the federal jail, prisoners receive two days served for every day of work, but no such credit exists for federal prisoners, and they must serve their full time.

Brown said Epps never had access to any keys and the jail doors are operated electronically. He also said all prisoners must eat food provided by the jail unless given a special diet by a physician, and Epps did not have a special diet. He also refutes the claims that Epps had a private room and said the only private rooms are solitary confinement.

As a matter of fact, famous female serial killer Nannie Doss was Epps' cellmate. Nannie Doss, also known as "The Giggling Granny" or "The Giggling Nanny" or "The Lonely Heart Killer" or "The Black Widow" was once dubbed a "self-made widow."

Doss was responsible for the deaths of 11 people in a span of 30 years. After her fifth husband died in 1954, Doss admitted to killing four husbands, two sisters, two children, a grandson, her mother, and a mother-in-law.

Through asphyxia and poisoning, Doss had 11 murders to her name, but her name is rarely mentioned with the world's worst serial killers.

The Queen of the Bootleggers and the Black Widow were roomies, and they were in starch contrast to each other. Cleo Epps loved children and would never harm a hair on their heads. She went out of her way to make sure children had everything they needed to survive and was a mother to just about everyone she met.

Doss killed men, women, and children without any regret or remorse. The two women did have one thing in common: the love of very bad men.

Doss was only convicted in the murder of her fifth husband, Samuel Doss, by arsenic poisoning. The Doss family was living in Tulsa, Oklahoma at the time of Samuel's death, and Nannie Doss pleaded guilty to his murder, receiving a life sentence in 1955. The state of Oklahoma did not pursue the death penalty because of her gender, and she died of Leukemia 10 years later in the Oklahoma State Penitentiary in McAlester, Oklahoma.

On Wednesday, August 16, 1955, Cleo Epps was released from prison after serving a six-month sentence for the importation of liquor into dry Oklahoma. She actually served five months, getting one-month allowance for good behavior.

Her five-month stint was not without controversy, including the "run of the jail" accusations. The controversy started the day she entered the jail. On her first day, Epps, who was working as a bail bondsman, tried to assure a $20,000 bond for Chicago hoodlum Rubin Schetsky, who had previously been convicted of burglary and assault with intent to kill.

The court refused to accept Epps' bond for Schetsky.

She served her time, and, five months later, at 12:01 a.m. Wednesday, August 17, 1955, Cleo Epps walked out of the Tulsa County jail a free woman. Some women stay the night in jail, waiting until the morning to be released. Epps wasted no time, walking out of facility exactly one minute past her release date.

About a month later, The Federal Bureau of Prisons gave the Tulsa County jail a clean bill of health for handling prisoners on a non-preferential basis. All of Roberts' claims about Epps and the jail were said to be unfounded, according to the Bureau of Prisons.

A bureau representative said, "There was nothing to indicate anything contrary to good prison practices." That closed the book on the jail complaints, and Epps was now a free woman, again.

Epps was free, but she wasn't free of controversy or criminal activity.

Trouble just seemed to find Cleo Epps, and other than bootlegging, it was hard to pin anything on her. Sometimes, her cronies did all of the dirty work.

In 1958, Epps' truck was temporarily confiscated by the Tulsa County Sheriff's Office and held as evidence in connection with an attempted theft in Broken Arrow, a town that borders Tulsa to the east.

On Sunday, March 9, 1958, Tulsa County deputies surprised three men who were loading construction materials onto a truck near a house being built in Broken Arrow Heights, a housing addition in south Broken Arrow. After the men saw deputies, they fled on foot, and despite several warning shots from officers, the men kept running.

During a quick investigation, the truck was found to be registered to Cleo Epps. She was interviewed the following Monday and claims the last time she saw her truck it was parked in the driveway of a home she was building in Sapulpa on Epps Road.

Window frames and screens were found in the back of her truck, and officers went to the house that Epps said was under construction, however, it was already equipped with window frames and screens. The house was almost completely finished.

Epps Road and Epps Addition are located seven miles northeast of Sapulpa near the Creek and Tulsa County lines just off of U.S. Route 66.

Epps said the truck must have been stolen and had no idea it was gone until deputies showed up at her front door to question her.

After a two-week investigation, Epps had to answer some new, tougher questions. Police arrested three suspects -- Romey Lee Wilcoxon, W.L. "Chief" Sanders, and Alonzo Scott Painter -- in connection with the "stolen" truck and building materials in Broken Arrow.

On March 25, 1958, Epps was questioned again by police, and the questions were turning into accusations. After checking records, investigators found out that, for years, Epps had been posting bonds for two of the three suspects -- Wilcoxon and Sanders.

Records show that Epps posted, and lost, a $3,000 bond for Wilcoxon because he skipped bail, however, she posted another bond for him a few years later after an arrest in Shawnee, Oklahoma. In 1956, Epps posted a $2,000 bond for Sanders in Wagoner County.

During the investigation, officers searched Epps' properties and found stolen television sets and hi-fi stereo equipment that was estimated to be worth around $15,000.

Epps told officers that Wilcoxon left the stolen items at her house.

The three suspects were also arrested in Ada, Oklahoma on a charge of burglary with explosives in the attempted safe burglary of an Ada supermarket. The store burned at a loss of $75,000. The three were also charged with burglaries in Tulsa, Oklahoma City, Shawnee, and Coal County.

Four years after her 1955 conviction, prohibition was repealed in the United States in 1959, and grain alcohol was legal again, but that didn't mean Epps was out of business. She kept ties with the Dixie Mafia and still had customers that bought her illegal hooch. However, Epps expanded her other operations and became a fence for thieves and robbers. If someone had loot, they needed to unload, Epps was always interested, and she offered a fair price.

During her more than 30 years as a bootlegger, Epps was smart enough to purchase property, land, businesses, and build houses.

By 1970, Epps' estate was valued at just under $750,000; she had 13 real estate properties that totaled just over 1,500 acres valued at $250,000 and 34 mortgages and notes valued at $432,000. That did not include the amount of cash she had at her house or on her property.

Epps would buy land and build houses to sell or rent. She would also help with the construction of those houses, overseeing the work, even swinging a hammer herself. Epps was strong and wasn't afraid of hard work.

There was an Epps road and even an Epps housing addition that had several houses on a dead-end street. She lived in one of the houses in Epps Addition, located east just off of West 81st St and New Sapulpa Road (Route 66). It was only a few miles away from West Tulsa. Epps Road still exists to this day and is also called South 67th West Avenue.

She would build a house and live in it until it sold, or she rented it out. Epps would often stay in a mobile trailer until a house was built, and she would then move into the house after it was completed. Sometimes, the houses were sold immediately, and she would start on a new one.

Epps physically helped build every single house, and when she sold a house, she carried the note on it. Epps didn't need a bank to do business, and she never wrote anything down. She did all of the math in her head, and she knew exactly what everyone owed her. She collected the mortgages herself at the beginning of every month.

It was not uncommon for Epps to have stacks of cash on her kitchen counter at the first of the month or to have mason jars full of cash in her cupboards. On the night of her death, Epps reportedly had thousands of dollars in cash on her counter that hadn't been put in jars or deposited somewhere.

Some people say she had several barns full of whiskey that was already made or in the process of being made.

Epps was generous with her money, her time, and her possessions.

On a 1953 hunting trip with friends in Idaho, the group became snowed-in and couldn't leave the cabin, which she owned. Epps shot a moose, believing it was a deer, and told local rangers that she would turn the animal over to a charitable organization. However, she couldn't leave the cabin due to the weather conditions and received permission to use the animal's meat to feed hunters that were in the same predicament. She was able to feed around 35 hunters that could make their way to her cabin.

But the hunters weren't the only ones to benefit from her hunting abilities. Epps often shot wild game that was indigenous to the north and couldn't be found in Oklahoma, bringing back elk, bear, large deer, antelope, possum, and other exotic creatures. Then, she hosted barbecues for the neighborhood. The potluck dinners made with exotic meats were free, but everyone brought a side dish.

Epps also owned a motel in Town West that had a swimming pool. During the hot Oklahoma summers, she would invite the neighborhood kids to swim in the motel pool for free.

There were a lot of Dixie Mafia members that stayed there for free, as well.

She loved children and loved being surrounded by them all the time. She had nieces and nephews that were always at her house playing games, reading books, or baking cookies. Whether it was the loss of her son at infancy or her years as a schoolteacher, Epps loved being around children, and she was a proud aunt to every one of them.

Epps did eventually become a mother, unofficially.

She took in a runaway who came to her looking for work. At age 11, Carl Main became Epps' foster son, and she tried to make sure he wanted for nothing. Although he was never officially adopted, she treated Carl like he was her own son -- the son she never got to have.

Main was from Arkansas, and when Epps took him in, she contacted his parents who told her "just keep him." Apparently, his family had more children than they could take care of and were very poor.

His parents said, "keep him" and that's exactly what she did.

Epps also rubbed elbows with some famous people because Epps was famous in her own right.

As a child, Epps' second cousin Sue Rush McInnis would spend countless hours at Epps' house. Epps' mother Daisy and Sue's grandmother were sisters and Sue was 40 years younger than Epps. Sue affectionately called Epps "Aunt Cleo."

One day, when Sue was in grade school, she was at her Aunt Cleo's house when a beautiful white convertible started down the driveway. When it got closer, Sue could see it was a white 1958 Cadillac Convertible with bright red interior.

Driving the convertible was a handsome -- some would say gorgeous -- man with flowing blonde hair and a golden-brown tan. He was very muscular and looked like a movie star from California. He was about 5-foot-9 and weighed around 215 pounds of pure muscle.

Sue couldn't really hear the conversation, but she could tell her Aunt Cleo and the blonde man were quite sweet on each other.

He drove away and that was it.

Years later, Sue found out the man in the Cadillac was professional wrestling icon George Raymond Wagner, also known as "Gorgeous George."

She was eventually told that her Aunt Cleo and Gorgeous George had a brief romance, and he was in town that day for a wrestling match.

It wasn't uncommon for Epps to hang out with wrestlers. She owned a second motel called "The Deville" and most of the professional wrestlers stayed there while performing in Tulsa. It's also no secret that wrestlers liked to drink, and Epps could help them with that, too.

*****

In 1966, Epps was arrested again and charged with two counts of aiding and abetting in the sale of untaxed spirits, and one count of conspiracy, involving illicit liquor operations. She was charged with seven other defendants, George Doty, Raymond O. Jones, Jerry Lee Holiday, Billy Ray Adams, Harold Ben Marley, Albert Hill, and her brother Sam Gilbert.

It was alleged to be a multi-million-dollar operation that flooded the Tulsa and Sapulpa areas with thousands of gallons of whiskey a month.

The arrests stemmed from several surveillance missions by the Alcohol, Tobacco and Firearms Agency (ATF).

On March 30, 1965, Sam Gilbert, Epps' older brother, purchased 10,000 pounds of sugar from Gordon Hixson with money Epps gave him. Hixson arranged the sale through a warehouse in Fort Smith, Arkansas. On April 8, 1965, an additional 12,000 pounds of sugar was purchased through the same grocer and warehouse, but Gilbert denies any involvement in this transaction. To prove Gilbert's involvement in the second transaction, Alcohol and Tobacco Tax investigators testified that on April 8, 1965, they followed a red Ford truck traveling along Highway 64 away from Fort Smith, Arkansas, toward Warner, Oklahoma. Following two or three car-lengths behind the truck, the investigators were able to determine that the truck contained numerous sacks of White Gold sugar.

Sugar is one of the main ingredients in the production of moonshine and obtaining that much sugar can mean only one thing.

Investigator Robert M. Finley saw the truck enter a weigh station near Warner, and a 1964 maroon Chevrolet containing two people pulled off alongside the road just past the station, obviously waiting for the truck.

After a few minutes, the maroon Chevrolet drove off down the road towards Warner but pulled into a drive-in parking area. The car stayed there for a short while and then drove back toward the weigh station. Ten or fifteen minutes later, the car returned to the drive-in parking area.

The investigators, which included John L. Day, recognized Gilbert as the driver of the truck. Cleo Epps and Raymond O. Jones were the occupants in the impatient maroon Chevrolet.

Gilbert also made large sugar purchases on March 30, 1965, and April 8, 1965, and on the latter purchase, Epps and Jones were in tow.

The authorities could not link Gilbert to any of the whiskey sales, but they were convinced he was purchasing the items needed to make the whiskey, which led to the conspiracy charge. While Gilbert's sugar purchases and association with Epps and Jones may be sufficient to create suspicion, it did not lead to a charge of selling untaxed spirits.

Gilbert was only charged with conspiracy, and all of the defendants, except Hill, were convicted of conspiracy.

During the four-day trial, 50 witnesses were called to the stand, and U.S. District Attorney Hugh V. Schaefer characterized Cleo Epps as the "queen of the moonshine operation." In a fiery and emotional summation, Schaefer said Epps operated the whiskey ring from her motel, the Western Capri.

"This was an organization, and Cleo Epps was the queen of the operation. From her vantage point at the motel, she worked those in the setup like puppets on a string. She talked to whiskey salesmen, and others -- the distillers and manufacturers of this non-tax paid whiskey," Schaefer said.

Epps' attorney, Everett S. Collins, said Epps was not a part of the illegal alcohol ring and claimed she had to take out a loan to buy the Western Capri Motel. If she was the head of this operation, she could have just paid cash for the motel.

"They know she purchased the motel with a loan from the Small Business Administration. Cleo is a hard-working woman. Anything she has she built and made with her own hands. She is always helping people," Collins said to the court.

Schaefer rebutted with: "Mrs. Epps probably used the profits from the moonshine business to make the loan payments on her motel."

All but two of the defendants decided not to testify on their own behalf. Only Epps and Gilbert testified during the trial, and that came back to bite Epps.

The prosecutor told the jury during his final argument that Epps and Gilbert were the only ones to attempt to refute the government's charges by testifying under oath, and since the other defendants refused to testify, they must be guilty. He said the government presented its case and without their testimony to rebut it, they are guilty and there was no other reasonable conclusion.

However, a defendant has the right not to testify, and the law states that a refusal to testify cannot be a determining factor in guilt.

Under the Fifth Amendment of the Constitution, a defendant has the absolute right to not testify at trial, which could result in self-incrimination. When a defendant decides not to testify, the judge generally gives this instruction to the jury in some form, "The fact that the defendant did not testify is not a fact from which any inference unfavorable to the defendant may be drawn."

The prosecutor made a mistake by trying to sway the jury with the fact that most of the defendants did not testify.

On Friday, May 27, 1966, a jury of five women and seven men deliberated for around five hours before returning with a verdict. Cleo Epps and eight male defendants were found guilty of operating a multi-million-dollar whiskey ring in the Tulsa area. Sentencing was scheduled for June 14 in front of U.S. District Judge Allen Barrow, the same judge that heard the case.

Epps was facing a possible 10-year prison sentence and a $20,000 fine.

Before sentencing, Epps addressed the court and said she never had anything to do with moonshine whiskey and had not violated liquor laws since 1952.

"I admit violating liquor laws before 1952," she told the court. "But I've never had anything to do with non-tax liquor since that time."

On Tuesday, June 14, 1966, all were sentenced, and Epps was given an 18-month prison sentence and a $2,000 fine. Epps has always maintained that she never ventured into the moonshine business only participating in whiskey importation.

Her brother, Samuel Gilbert, was sentenced to six months and a $1,000 fine, Doty was given concurrent three-year terms on three counts of selling whiskey, $1,000 fine for possession, and five years probation on the conspiracy.

Jones received four concurrent three-year terms, a $500 fine, and three years probation for conspiracy.

Adams was handed 18 months in prison and two years probation, Holliday was sentenced to two years in prison and two years of probation, and Marley was given 18 months in prison.

Hill was the only defendant who didn't appeal his conviction and sentence of five-years probation.

After the verdict was read, Epps' brother, Samuel Gilbert, and two Tulsa newsmen scuffled in the alley behind the Federal Building, resulting in an assault charge for Gilbert.

Gilbert and Epps were walking to their cars still reeling from the fresh guilty verdicts when television cameramen Bob Gregory and Mike Miller attempted to film the two in the alley. Gilbert and Epps were covering their faces with newspapers as they left the building, and Gilbert attacked the two journalists.

Gregory, of KTUL Channel 8, and Miller of KOTV Channel 6, said Gilbert began swinging his fists at them, and he grabbed Gregory's $800 video camera and smashed it on the ground.

This wasn't Gilbert's first attempt at stopping the cameramen from doing their jobs. During the trial, a month earlier, Miller and another newsman attempted to take Epps' picture when Gilbert pulled a knife on the two and threatened them if they tried to take any more pictures.

In a twist of fate and a big mistake by the prosecution, all of the guilty verdicts were eventually overturned. However, the state appealed the Epps decision and her overturned conviction was then overturned. Epps was again guilty of a moonshine conspiracy charge.

The catch-22 for Epps and Gilbert was they decided to testify to rebut the government's claims; therefore, the prosecutor's inappropriate instructions to the jury did not apply to them.

Epps took her case all the way to the 10th U.S. Circuit of Appeals where her attorney, Thomas A. Wallace, made several arguments, including that Epps' conviction should be overturned because her co-defendants had their convictions overturned and that several wiretaps were illegal under the Fourth Amendment of the Constitution.

The government was permitted, over her attorney's objection, to introduce into evidence several tape recordings of telephone conversations between Epps and Charles Reese Walters, an undercover Alcohol Tax Unit agent. These "wiretaps" were obviously made with the consent of Agent Walter but unbeknownst to Epps. That evidence constituted a substantial part of the government's case against Epps, and her attorneys argued that it violated her rights under the Fourth Amendment unreasonable search and seizure.

Epps claimed that agent Walters, who used the name "Charlie Shaw" while undercover, began bothering her with constant phone calls about whiskey and even mentioned George Doty several times. She said she received so many phone calls that she started "fibbing" to Walters about her involvement in the whiskey business.

Walters even visited Epps at the Western Capri Motel as "Charlie Shaw," but she told Walters she was running a legitimate business and had nothing to do with whiskey anymore. She also claimed that she didn't own the Western Capri until December of 1965, buying it at a Sheriff's auction.

Epps also refuted the accusation that she bought 70 empty plastic gallon jugs from Walters, but the agent testified that Epps paid $7 for the jugs for the purposes of making and transporting moonshine.

She also said she did not own a home at 7832 E. King Street in Tulsa where agents said moonshine was sold. Epps owned the house at one time but said she sold it to a man named Charles Merchant, who eventually left because he couldn't make the payments. Technically, Epps still owned the house, but she claimed to have no knowledge of any moonshine business being operated from that house.

However, the courts ruled the taped conversations were admissible.

But, two years later, in 1968, the 10th U.S. Circuit Court of Appeals ruled such recordings or "bugged conversations" could not be used as evidence.

The government appealed the decision to vacate Epps' conviction and won, but Epps appealed their appeal. Her appeal was denied, but she had more appeals, and she remained out of jail without bond.

The other defendants started serving their various sentences toward the end of April 1966.

Things didn't slow down for Epps during her appeals in 1968. Epps was involved in a shooting at one of her motels -- The Deville.

On Saturday, April 27, there was a disturbance at The Deville, located at 5550 W. Skelly Drive, and motel desk clerk, Paul Shipman was forced to play security guard, which was just part of the job in that part of town.

At around 1 a.m., Shipman was sitting behind the counter in the lobby, watching the minutes tick off the clock when he noticed a commotion outside.

Two men and one woman were attempting to break in to one of the motel rooms.

Shipman was armed with his own .25 caliber pistol, but he was outnumbered, and he needed to call Cleo Epps to find out how to handle the situation. The Deville was located in Town West, near the Creek and Tulsa County lines and the motel guests were often sketchy. Shipman didn't know whether or not the three each had guns or if they were unarmed.

He called Epps, and, armed with a .22 rifle and Shipman's pistol, the two met at the motel and headed for the room.

Shipman told police he confronted the three suspects -- Milan Dwayne Mills, 21, Tommy Oliver Brixley, 21, and Diane Thompson, 21 -- but the two men attacked him and took the rifle away from him. When Mills pointed the rifle at Shipman, the clerk pulled the .25 from his pocket and fired a bullet into Mills' stomach. There was no mention of the woman attacking Shipman.

Thompson and Brixley grabbed Mills off the ground and carried him a short distance before his legs started churning, and the three suspects headed down South 49th Avenue. They were arrested only minutes later.

Shipman told the officers he shot Mills, and all three suspects were taken to jail, including Mills.

At around 6 a.m. Saturday morning, Mills was sitting in a jail cell at the Tulsa County jail with a bullet hole in his stomach. After numerous attempts to alert jailers of his injury, Mills was not having any luck, and he did the only thing he could do. Mills called for medical help from a phone at the jail.

Mills called the sheriff's office and told the dispatcher he was "wounded and bleeding."

The suspect was then transported to Hillcrest Medical Center to be treated for a gunshot wound to the abdomen. Mills did not have a bullet hole in his shirt, causing some confusion, and it's why officers missed the injury.

Police surmise that Mills raised his arms during the struggle with Shipman, exposing his stomach. Shipman then fired the gun, striking Mills in the midsection. He lowered his arms, and the bullet wound was covered by his shirt.

The Tulsa Tribune said officers claim Mills refused medical treatment.

Mills was no stranger to crime, and he wasn't really supposed to be out of prison. Mills was paroled from the Oklahoma State Penitentiary a year earlier. He served less than a year of his seven-year sentence after a conviction for burglary and assault.

On February 1966, Mills broke into the house of Gordon McKeague and beat the homeowner with a hammer.

Only ten months into his sentence, Mills was paroled on the one-year anniversary of the crime. Chief

County Prosecutor Pat Williams was upset about the parole and said Mills had not been in prison long enough for the crime committed.

Mills was released, but if Judge W. Lee Johnson had heeded Williams' warning, Mills would have been in prison at the time of the attempted break-in at The Deville. He wasn't scheduled for release until April of 1969.

Epps' involvement in the shooting, if there was any, was left out of any newspaper article about the event. The newspaper clippings just mention she went to the motel with Shipman and the guns.

CHAPTER FOUR
Stomping Grounds

Cleo Epps made Sapulpa and West Tulsa her home, and certain members of the Dixie Mafia seemed to always be in the area, making it their safe haven. With Epps' properties, motels, the Avalon Steakhouse, and access to Interstate 44, U.S. Route 75, U.S. Route 66, and the Turner Turnpike, it was easy to hide out or get out of town in a hurry.

Interstate 44 started in 1958 which basically linked Texas to Oklahoma City, and Oklahoma City to Tulsa, and Tulsa to Missouri, technically running southwest to northeast. I-44 is a 328-mile road that runs through Cotton, Comanche, Grady, McClain, Cleveland, Oklahoma, Lincoln, Creek, Tulsa, Rogers, Mayes, Craig, and Ottawa counties.

The Turner Turnpike opened in 1953 and is the state's oldest turnpike. It's only 86 miles long and turns into Interstate 44. It was named after former Oklahoma Governor Roy J. Turner, who was the driving force in the construction of the toll road that would connect the state's two biggest cities – Oklahoma City and Tulsa.

U.S. Route 75 (also known as Highway 75) is a 1,200-mile highway that runs north and south straight through Oklahoma, linking the state to Texas and Kansas. The highway actually runs from Dallas, Texas all the way to Canada, going through Oklahoma, Kansas, Nebraska, Iowa, and Minnesota.

U.S. Route 66 is a 2,400-mile stretch of road from Chicago, Illinois to Santa Monica, California, and it runs right through Sapulpa, Oklahoma, which has been tabbed "The Heart of Route 66." The Route 66 Museum is also located in Sapulpa, and there is a foot race called "The Bunion Derby," that started in 1928 and runs the length of the highway. The very first race was won by Oklahoman Andy Payne. The race, also known as the "Trans-American Footrace," goes from California to New York and originally took 84 days to complete.

All of these roads were, more than likely, used by Epps and the Dixie Mafia for their bootlegging operation, committing crimes in other states, or fleeing the heat brought on them for their local crimes.

West Tulsa

West Tulsa is the area of Tulsa located in the west part of the city of Tulsa, Oklahoma and includes several communities located in different counties and cities like Berryhill, Oakhurst, Red Fork, Carbondale, Crystal City, and Garden City. It's located to the west and south of the Arkansas River and includes parts of Sapulpa, Sand Springs, and Tulsa.

In 1907, West Tulsa became an incorporated town and was annexed by the city of Tulsa two years later in 1909.

Southwest Boulevard is the most popular road in West Tulsa, originally called Quanah Avenue, and is accessed off of Highway 75.

Town West is home to the Oaks Country Club, the now defunct Avalon Steakhouse, Camp Loughridge -- a Christian Summer Camp -- several oil refineries, numerous churches, the Burlington Northern Santa Fe (BNSF) railway, and several schools.

Daniel Webster High School and Berryhill High School are considered a part of West Tulsa along with several middle and elementary schools.

In the 1920s, West Tulsa had one of the first amusement parks in the area that had a Ferris wheel, dance hall, carousel, boat rides, and, at one point, the infamous Zingo, a wooden roller coaster. It closed and eventually reopened as "Crystal City." It stayed in business until a fire forced its closure in 1956. The area became a shopping center with a bowling alley and is still known as Crystal City.

The Zingo was eventually relocated to Bell's Amusement Park, a park that opened in 1951 and stayed open until 2006. Bell's was located on the Tulsa State Fairgrounds. The Zingo was the main attraction at the park, along with spook house, Phantasmagoria.

Town West

There is a shopping center between West Tulsa and Sapulpa called the "Town West Shopping Center," and that part of town is known as Town West. In 2004, the city of Sapulpa annexed Town West, expanding Sapulpa's borders and tax revenue.

When the Sapulpa city council annexed the area, it was nothing more than several low-rent motels that charged by the hour, a sex toy shop, a grocery store, gas stations, a truck stop and truck wash, and a lumber yard. Epps once owned two motels in Town West, The Deville and the Western Capri Motel.

Town West is located on the west side of I-44 and north of the Turner Turnpike gate. There are restaurants, hotels, and gas stations on the east side of the interstate, as well.

Tulsa

Tulsa is Oklahoma's second-largest city behind Oklahoma City, and it's located in the northeast part of the state, adjacent to the Arkansas River. Located in Tulsa County, Tulsa is the county seat. The city was started in the late 1820s with the removal of the Creek Indians from Georgia and Alabama. The Creek and Lower Creek Indians settled in what is known as Tulsa, but the railroad and the oil boom set a course for Tulsa to become a major city.

By the 1890s, Tulsa had churches, businesses, a depot, hotels, saloons, a bank, a Masonic Lodge, and much more. The discovery of oil at Red Fork in 1901 basically started it all, and oil was then found in the neighboring city of Glenpool four years later.

When oil was found in Glenpool, it became the nation's top producer of oil, and Ida Glenn No. 1 produced 75-barrels a day of "light and sweet" oil.

Tulsa then proclaimed to be the "Oil Capital of the World." In 1907, Oklahoma became a state, and Tulsa already had around 7,200 residents.

Just when Tulsa was on top of the world, that world came crashing down on May 31, 1921 when a race riot destroyed the predominantly-black part of the city. In less than 24 hours, around 40-square blocks of Tulsa's black community were destroyed after a young black man, Diamond Dick Rowland, was accused of assaulting a white girl, Sarah Page, in an elevator.

A white mob wanted Rowland lynched and showed up to the jail to do so. A group of black men also showed up at the jail to protect Rowland. The two groups squared off, shots were fired, and all hell broke loose.

The death toll is still a mystery, but there have been many guesses at the number of black and white men killed. Some estimates have been too high, and some too low.

Greenwood or "The Black Wall Street" would never really be the same again.

Despite the darkest day in the state's history, which is rarely taught in Oklahoma history classes, Tulsa kept thriving, attracting big businesses and industry, creating infrastructure, and building interstate travel and turnpikes.

For years, oil was a big part of downtown Tulsa and several oil barons had built skyscrapers for office buildings. There were supporting companies like equipment suppliers, banks, insurers, and hotels. Utility companies also started sprouting up all over downtown Tulsa.

By 1930, over 800 oil companies had offices in the Tulsa area, and, through the 1970s, the Tulsa World daily newspaper had four or five pages dedicated to the oil industry.

It's been reported the John Sinclair, of Sinclair Oil, Frank Phillips, of Phillips Petroleum, J. Paul Getty, of the Getty Oil Company, and Bill Skelly, of Skelly Oil Company, received their start in the oil business in Glenpool, Oklahoma

By the 1980s, Oklahoma experienced an oil bust, and a lot of oil companies went bankrupt. Some of the buildings that housed oil companies were re-purposed or razed to make way for other more lucrative businesses and even parking lots.

As of 2017, Tulsa has a population of over 400,000 people.

Sapulpa

The city of Sapulpa started as a trading post around 1850 established by a full-blood Lower Creek Indian named "Chief James Sapulpa" who was a member of the Kasihita tribe in Osocheetown, Alabama. He was Sapulpa's first official settler when Oklahoma was still Indian Territory.

Sapulpa's trading post was built near the confluence of Polecat and Rock Creeks, and the Pacific and Atlantic railroads expanded and laid track through the area in the 1880s, right past the trading post. In 1889, a post office was built and given the name "Sapulpa Station."

The town was incorporated in 1889, around nine years before statehood, and the Euchee Mission Boarding School was established in 1894 to teach Indian children.

When oil was discovered in Glenpool, six miles southeast of Sapulpa, and the town grew almost overnight. By the 1920s, the town had around 20,000 residents with four glass plants, two brick plants, and many other thriving businesses. Frankhoma Pottery, a company that made sculptures and dinnerware, popped up in the early 1930s and eventually became a tourist attraction for the city. It was located on Frankhoma Road, which was named after the company founder John Frank, who was a professor of ceramics and the University of Oklahoma.

Sapulpa is the county seat of Creek County.

CHAPTER FIVE
Judge Fred Nelson's car Bombing

On the morning of Tuesday, August 25, 1970, District Judge Fred S. Nelson was leaving his house to do his civic duty, but not the normal everyday duties he did as a sitting district judge in Tulsa County. Judge Nelson was leaving his house in Tulsa to go to his polling place to vote in the primary elections.

His name was on the ballot, and he was going to cast his vote like any other red-blooded American. In 1970, courthouses were closed on Election Day, allowing city hall employees, lawyers, and judges the opportunity to vote, and Nelson was taking full advantage.

The 41-year old judge lived in an upper-class Tulsa neighborhood that sat adjacent to Thomas Edison High School. His house was located off of 41st Street between Yale and Harvard at 3944 S. Evanston Avenue

Before being elected as a district judge, Nelson worked for Gulf Oil, was an attorney for the U.S. Interior Department, and served as assistant U.S. attorney in Tulsa.

Nelson was a native of Tulsa and received his bachelor's degree and law degrees from the University of Tulsa. He also attended the University of Oklahoma Law School.

Nelson and his wife, Ann, had been married since 1951 and they had four children -- one boy and three girls. The Nelson men were definitely outnumbered. Ann, a stunningly beautiful woman, exuded class and grace and she always dressed in the latest fashions. Her mother, Margaret, was the founder of Tulsa's iconic "Margo's Gift Shop," located in the Utica Square Shopping Center, and Ann and her mother worked together for years.

The Nelson's worked hard to provide a warm and loving home for their four children.

The sunny August morning was nearing noon. At just around 11 a.m., Judge Nelson walked from his front door towards the family car, a 1969 blue Oldsmobile station wagon, parked in front of the house. He sat down in the wagon, grabbed the car key from the floorboard and placed the key in the ignition, turning the ignition switch.

A horrific explosion lifted the car up off the ground, and a flash of light, flames, and pressure filled the car.

The light blue station wagon was smoking and still on fire when Nelson crawled out of the vehicle. Most of the damage was done to the front driver's side of the car where he was sitting. The hood was completely blown off, exposing the mangled engine, and the driver's side door was barely hanging from the hinges. One of the wagon's hubcaps lay on the front lawn around 30 yards from the car and smoke could be seen floating from the metal wheel covering.

The blast radius was around 100-feet, and the garage door was warped and cracked from the heat of the blast. Several of the wooden shingles on the Nelson house were damaged or blown completely off.

Nelson's body was thrown upward and back during the blast, and the wagon filled with thick black smoke. Nelson couldn't see, and he immediately grabbed the point of impact on his body, which was his stomach and chest, and what he felt was terrifying.

At the time, Nelson was worried about his stomach and he didn't notice the damage to his foot, which was extensive.

Douglas Christopher Packard, a 14-year old high school student, was in the parking lot of Tulsa's Thomas Edison High School, walking toward the main building. He heard an unbelievable explosion behind him, and he turned in time to see the blue hood of a station wagon fly more than 100-feet in the air.

Packard ran towards the blast to see if anyone was hurt, and he came upon a sight that looked like it was straight out of a war movie. The 14-year old ran up to the car and saw Judge Nelson sitting on the ground. He saw pools of blood forming under the judge and before he could ask the judge what happened, Nelson said in a weak voice, "Please call an ambulance."

Still in shock, Packard was getting ready to rush to a neighbor's house to ask to use the phone when Nelson calmly said, "Son, do you have a wet rag?" Nelson was out of breath like he had just run a marathon. He was confused but knew he needed help.

Packard replied, "No, I don't, sir. Hold on, I'm gonna get help."

Packard ran back towards the high school. Nelson closed his eyes and passed out, losing consciousness. The only thing keeping Nelson awake up to that point was the rush of adrenaline he received from living through the blast. That adrenaline slowly wore off, and Nelson's body went limp.

Judge Nelson's intestines were now on the outside of his body. The blast ripped a hole in his stomach and his guts were visible. A large piece of metal believed to be a cross strut of the firewall did the most damage and that injury was the most concerning. Nelson had to hold his guts in his stomach until medical personnel arrived at the scene, which was between five and ten minutes after the first call for an ambulance.

Saint Francis, Saint John, and Hillcrest Hospitals were all less than five miles away in two different directions.

Nelson's seatbelt strap was sliced through, and, more than likely, it was the strap that slowed the large piece of metal from severing his spine.

Across the street in the Edison High School Building, assistant principal Roger Smith was getting ready for the lunch bell when he heard the explosion. Smith looked out of his window and saw the smoke coming from the neighborhood just across the street. He grabbed his coat, yelled for his secretary to call the police, and ran out of the door towards the smoke. At a full sprint, Assistant Principal Smith squeezed through the rows of parked cars in the parking lot and darted across the street. He ran towards the blast site and saw one of his students running from the scene.

Smith wasn't there long before the ambulance arrived, and Nelson was then taken to Saint Francis Hospital, located at 6161 S. Yale in Tulsa. The hospital was just under three miles away, and, with lights and sirens blaring, the ambulance rushed down 41st Street, turning south on Harvard Avenue and then east on 61st Street, turning south onto Yale.

When Nelson arrived, he was rushed directly into surgery.

The Tulsa Tribune, an afternoon newspaper, published an article immediately after the bombing, going with what little information they had gathered in a short period of time.

"BULLETIN: A surgeon at Saint Francis Hospital said at 2:15 p.m. today, Judge Fred Nelson was in "very serious" condition with extensive injuries in the abdomen. He reportedly had lost a lot of blood, and also suffered a broken foot in this morning's explosion. A number of metal fragments, one termed sizable, were removed from his abdomen. Surgery, which started at 11:40 a.m., was expected to continue until later afternoon."

While in surgery, doctors removed metal fragments of various sizes, and the judge needed blood transfusions due to the loss of blood at the scene and in the ambulance. Nelson was in surgery for over three hours. A spokesman for the hospital told newspapers that Nelson was also suffering from "generalized burns and lacrations of the body."

Dr. Donald L. Brewer headed the team of four surgeons that were in the fight to save Nelsons life and said a fist-size piece of metal and numerous smaller pieces were removed from his abdomen and legs. A large hole was also blown in his abdominal wall, and some of that wall was completely blown away by the blast.

During the surgery, parts of the intestine were removed, and damage to the urinary tract was repaired. Portions of the judge's right foot needed to be rebuilt.

Fire Marshall Roy Gann made the statement that the bomb was placed by a professional who knew exactly what he was doing.

The car's front grill had been blown away from the car, and the vent under the windshield was a crumpled mess and pushed into the glass. The bomb was placed on the driver's side of the car between the firewall and the engine and was meant to kill whoever turned the key.

It was an attempted assassination, and Tom Lester Pugh and Albert McDonald were suspected almost immediately.

Behind the mangled wagon, a wooden political sign leaned up against the Nelson's house. The sign was around 10-feet tall and was meant to be seen over the station wagon as people drove by the house. Painted with red and black lettering it read: "Retain Judge Nelson."

That's exactly what Pugh and McDonald were trying to prevent.

Judge Nelson was in critical condition but survived the attack and presiding judge Robert Simms ordered protection for all other county judges and ordered court clerks to review all of Judge Nelson's cases.

It was suspected that McDonald and Pugh, with the help of Arlis Delbert Self, made the car bomb and placed it under Judge Nelson's car, and the motive was political. The Dixie Mafia needed an ally on the bench, and old friend Charles Pope could be the ally they needed. Pope had represented both Pugh and McDonald in some of their previous criminal court cases.

District Attorney S.M. Buddy Fallis once said, "By the grace of God and the skill of a surgeon (Nelson) was saved."

Apparently, Judge Nelson wore a rather large belt buckle, and the explosion blew metal parts of the car towards Nelson, and his belt buckle deflected some of that metal. Often times, in a bombing, it's the shrapnel that does the most damage, but God was watching over Judge Nelson that day.

Charles Pope was a local lawyer and was considered a friend of Pugh and McDonald. Pope, a democrat, was running against Judge Nelson, a republican that was very popular in the community. His re-election was almost a sure-thing, and counting the votes was just a formality.

Jack Tharp was a third-party candidate, but basically had no bearing on the election.

The Tulsa County Bar Association put up $25,000 for the arrest and conviction of the bomber, or bombers, and the reward grew to $32,500. Several days later, the reward was $34,850 and a special bank account was opened to receive contributions. Tulsa businesses started giving and the reward fund grew larger and larger.

As he paced the floor while Nelson was in surgery, former Tulsa Mayor, James Hewgley, decided to put up $500 of his own money. People from all over the state were giving money as if they were sending a message to the culprits that violence and lawlessness would not be tolerated in Tulsa anymore.

Governor Dewey F. Bartlett, and his wife, Ann, arrived at the hospital during surgery.

A good friend of Nelson's, Bartlett was shocked by the news of the bombing.

"I am stunned by the bombing attack on Judge Nelson. It is unbelievable that such a thing could happen to one of our district judges, particularly a person like Judge Nelson, who is so highly respected. He is a close personal friend. Ann and I are praying for his speedy recovery. At my request, the state Crime Bureau is aiding in local law enforcement officers in the investigation of this vicious tragic attack."

The president of the Tulsa World, and World Publishing Company, donated $2,500 and KTUL-TV Channel 8 added $500. KVOO Radio, Carson-Wilson American Legion Post No. 1, First National Bank and Trust Co., and Farmers & Merchants Bank all pledged $1,000 each.

District Attorney Fallis was on the scene quicker than any other crime scene because he was already in the area. Fallis was playing golf at LaFortune Golf Course with Judge Bill Means. The golf course is only a few miles away from the Nelson home and just down the street from Saint Francis Hospital.

Fallis received a call about the bombing from Tulsa Police Chief Jack Purdy, and Fallis quickly jumped in his car and headed there. After looking over the crime scene, he headed back to his office and assembled his team. He was pouring over files and possible threats when he had a crazy idea.

While talking with members of his crew, Frank Thurman, who would eventually become Tulsa County Sheriff, and Donny Creighton, Fallis said, "This might sound like something out of Hollywood, but we need to talk to Jack Tharp and Charlie Pope. But maybe they know something since they're running in opposition to him for the spot."

They got a hold of Tharp by telephone, and he was very cooperative. He wanted to be as helpful as possible.

Pope did not.

The lawyer friend of career criminals McDonald and Pugh refused to talk to Fallis about Nelson's attack.

Minutes later, a different lawyer called Fallis' office and said, "Oh, he'll talk to you when he feels like he can do it, but he just doesn't feel right about this, right now."

That's when it appeared Pope might be indirectly involved, even unknowingly.

However, Pope did speak to the local newspapers saying he was "simply numb" and that he grieved for Nelson's family, but Nelson wasn't dead. Grief was generally reserved for death.

Tharp, the third-party candidate, spoke to the news and even called Fred Nelson by name. He said, "I am deeply shocked. My primary concern is that Fred makes a satisfactory recovery."

Former Head Football Coach at the University of Oklahoma, Bud Wilkinson, called Judge Nelson's wife, Ann, with words of encouragement. Wilkinson, who was an advisor to President Richard Nixon at the time, called from Washington D.C.

Not too long after the bombing, Jack McKenzie, an investigator and friend of Cleo Epps, called Thurman and told him he knew there was going to be a bombing.

"You knew?" Thurman said in shock.

McKenzie replied, "Well, no. I didn't know who was going to get bombed or where it was going to happen. I had some information that was given to me by a source that indicated that there was some dynamite that might be used in some kind of bombing."

That information led to a meeting with Fallis and Epps at her home. There, Fallis learned about Arlis Delbert Self's involvement in the bombing. Self was a well-known criminal in the southern United States, and he specialized in bomb-making. He spent some time at the Western Capri Motel, owned by Epps, and he allegedly showed McDonald how to make a bomb and secure it to a car.

McKenzie persuaded Self to talk to Fallis about the Nelson car bombing, and Self told the district attorney how he instructed McDonald and Pugh to make the bomb and how to put the bomb on a car. He eventually showed

Fallis where and how he taught the two, using a small piece of pipe and a small explosive.

Fallis then asked judge Bob Simms to impanel a grand jury to indict Pugh and McDonald, and now Self and Epps had to testify against their friends in the Nelson case.

The following day, a special police guard dog was posted outside of Nelson hospital room, and several other police guard dogs were sent to the Nelson home on Evanston Avenue

Near 59th and Harvard, a campaign sign read, "Vote For Judge Nelson," but was converted to a different type of sign for the injured judge. The "vote for" was repainted to read "get well," and the large sign now read, "Get Well Judge Nelson."

A "Help Fred Nelson Fund" was also created to help pay for the judge's medical and hospital bills that were going to be astronomical. He would have the ambulance ride, the multiple surgeries, the hospital stay, and weeks of therapy to pay for. The Tulsa Tribune set aside $1,000 and wanted to raise an additional $4,000, and met that goal, easily.

The day of the bombing, FBI explosive experts arrived at the crime scene and immediately started collecting bits and pieces of the car to send to Washington D.C. to be analyzed. The FBI was hoping to be able to link the evidence to the assailants. Their main goal was to determine the method of how the charge was triggered and the type of explosive used.

Bombers rarely change up their method of operations, sticking with what they know. A preliminary walk-through was performed on Wednesday, August 26, the day after the bombing, and more evidence was gathered, and preliminary information was given to local law enforcement. Other materials were sent to Washington D.C. for more testing.

The FBI did not want to say publicly that the bomb was the work of a "professional." An FBI official said, "Many people have had experience with explosives. For example, farmers use dynamite to blow out stumps when clearing pasture."

He had no idea just how right he was. Cleo Epps used dynamite to blow out stumps when clearing a pasture, and this was her dynamite.

Nelson won the primary by 70-percent of the republican vote by receiving 24,293 votes, and Pope received 6,230 on the democratic side. The judge refused to be intimidated. He stayed in the hospital for six weeks and returned home, and he returned to the bench the same week. He then easily defeated Pope in the general election.

During that time, Dist. Judge Robert D. Simms sent letters to members of the Tulsa Bar with a list of new security procedures for the courthouse.

Anyone entering a judge's outer office or chambers must first obtain permission from a bailiff, court clerk or the judge. Anyone unknown to the clerks must obtain clearance from the judge to enter the outer office. Attorney's must receive the same clearance for their clients to enter the judge's chambers, and deputy sheriffs may remain armed in the courtroom during criminal trials.

Nelson retired two years after the bombing in 1972, went into private practice in Tulsa, and was a partner in the firm of Hall, Estill, Hardwick, Gable, Golden, and Nelson.

While in private practice, Sue Rush McInnis's sister, Barbara Rush, interviewed for a job at Fred Nelson's law firm, working directly with the former judge. During the interview, Barbara said, "I need to tell you something. Cleo Epps is my cousin."

Nelson laughed and said, "That was a different time in my life."

She got the job.

Judge Nelson was first appointed a district judge in 1967 by Governor Bartlett after the state legislature created a new judgeship for Tulsa County. At the time, he was serving as a common plea jurist after being appointed in 1965. He won election to the post in 1966. He was assistant U.S. Attorney from 1958 to 1961 and then entered private practice. In 1962, he ran unsuccessfully for district court.

Judge Nelson died of an apparent heart attack Monday, July 27, 1987 at the age of 58. It was 17 years after a car bomb nearly killed him.

His beautiful wife, Ann, lived 27 more years but died after a four-year battle with melanoma. She died while vacationing in Seaside, Florida. Her last moments were spent just feet from the sea and sands that she loved. She was surrounded by all four children, their spouses and children. They sang songs, joined hands in prayer, and shared fond memories. Ann died holding Fred's wedding ring, the same ring she gave him on their wedding day. The inscription read, "One Life One Love."

The decision to kill Judge Nelson set in motion a series of murders. Those killings occurred to prevent Pugh and McDonald from being charged with the car bombing and attempted murder of the judge. By the time it was all over, there were three witnesses and three murders.

CHAPTER SIX
Bootlegging

In the south, bootleggers are folk heroes. Some are real and some aren't, but America holds a special place in its heart for the men and women that provided grain alcohol to people in a time when they couldn't get it otherwise.

One of the greatest college football coaches of all time was a bootlegger's boy. Former University of Oklahoma head coach, Barry Switzer, was raised in the home of an Arkansas bootlegger, his father, Frank Switzer, and Barry eventually found his way to Oklahoma where he won college football national championships in 1974, 1975, and 1985.

The fictional Dukes of Hazzard was a television show that aired on CBS from 1979 to 1985, telling the story of cousins Bo and Luke Duke, who were once convicted of running moonshine but gave up that life, and their uncle Jesse gave up making the hooch in return for the boys' freedom. They turned their lives around and spent the one-hour weekly show, thwarting Boss Hogg's money-making schemes while saving people of Hazzard County at the same time.

They were fighting the system like true modern-day Robin Hoods.

The moonshine-running, fast-car driving, police-evading, couldn't resist the ladies, multiple-time jail-escaping, couldn't carry guns while on probation, couldn't leave the county Duke boys were heroes.

NASCAR was born out of bootlegging, where runners transported moonshine under the cover of night during prohibitions near 15-year ban on alcohol. Spirits were outlawed thanks to the Eighteenth Amendment of the United States Constitution which established the prohibition of intoxicating liquors by declaring it illegal to produce, transport, or sell.

Bootleggers needed to outrun the law, and, sometimes, they needed to outrun each other. The "moonrunners" began modifying the engines of their coupes to make them faster. They needed to get some separation from law enforcement if they were being chased and having a "souped up" motor could do that.

Also known as the Volstead Act, the National Prohibition Act, tasked the U.S. Treasury Department with enforcement of the new restrictions and defined which "intoxicating liquors" were forbidden and which were excluded from Prohibition for medical and religious reasons. That's right – religious reasons.

Between 1920 and 1933, there were doctors all across the county that would write prescriptions for a pint of whiskey, for the right price. It was for medicinal purposes. Medicinal whiskey.

In that same time period, crime syndicates fought for a bigger piece of the illegal alcohol market, and it often turned bloody, resulting in countless murders. Gangs ruled major cities with an unrelenting fist and did whatever it took to gain as much territory as possible, and then they had to defend it. Illegal liquor sales were nearly impossible to enforce, and some officials chose not to, again, if the price was right.

The lack of enforcement is how the mafia got started and how a lot of immigrants were able to gain power in cities like New York and Chicago, using some of the same brutality they were fleeing from.

Some bootleggers and moonshiners not only needed faster cars to outrun law enforcement, they need bigger and more powerful guns to overpower the law, as well. It wasn't uncommon for them to have an arsenal of high-powered weapons.

There were separate liquor laws for Oklahoma and Indian territories. Oklahoma allowed the sale of alcohol, but Indian territories could not due to federal law and a touch of racism.

Statehood came in 1907, and, in 1919, Oklahoma ratified the 18th Amendment, which banned the production, importation, transportation, and sale of alcoholic beverages. Alcohol was a problem well before statehood and, it was addressed less than 15 years later.

In early 1933, Congress adopted a resolution proposing the 21st Amendment, repealing the 18th Amendment. It was ratified by the end of 1933, and prohibition came to an end.

Oklahoma adopted prohibition into its constitution in 1907, and the first case of legal beer wasn't delivered to Oklahoma until July of 1933. Liquor was still illegal but readily available. It basically poured in, mainly, from Arkansas and Missouri.

By 1933, beer was legal in Oklahoma, but there was still prohibition for beer, so to speak. Low-point beer was the only beer allowed in the state. Beer that was 6.0 or higher could not be sold. There were also weird laws that accompanied beer sales. Eventually, a higher-point beer could only be sold in liquor stores, but there couldn't be any refrigerated coolers in the liquor stores so the beer couldn't be consumed immediately. Lawmakers were hoping the beer would need to be taken home and chilled before consumption, and the stores couldn't be open on a Sunday.

When it comes to beer, Oklahoma was dry from 1907 to 1933, but only 3.2 low-point beer was allowed, starting in 1933.

On April 7, 1959, more than 700,000 Oklahomans turned out for a special election, and the liquor law was repealed by more than 80,000 votes. Legal whiskey was sold for the first time in Oklahoma on September 1, 1959.

When it comes to grain alcohol, Oklahoma was dry from 1907 to 1959, and when it comes to high-point beer, Oklahoma was sort of dry from 1907 to 2018. High-point beer and wine could finally be sold in gas stations and grocery stores 110 years after Oklahoma became a state.

Between statehood and 1959, bootlegging flourished, and farmers found out that they could use corn for something other than agriculture. All they needed was water, corn, yeast and sugar. They also needed a still and some patience. Moonshine starts with a mash that has a fermenting process. With a heat source and lots of containers to bottle, the "intoxicating spirits" were ready, and the moonshiners were ready to make money.

The first 35 percent of moonshine could be lethal due to the methanol content, but the rest is good for consumption. If it didn't kill you, it could cause serious health issues, including blindness.

Bootlegging wasn't a secret, and most of the bootleggers had business cards that simply read, "Call Jim, Day or Night" with a telephone number.

Doctors might not have made house calls, but bootleggers did. Just like the milkman each morning, a bootlegger could deliver any kind of whiskey right to your front door.

Some bootleggers tried to circumvent the law, thinking if they didn't actually receive money for the alcohol it wouldn't be a crime. In some cases, a thirsty customer would leave the money on the porch and go back inside the house. The moonshiner would leave the liquor and take the money. No money ever changed hands, technically. There was no transaction because it didn't occur face-to-face or hand-to-hand. It was just one guy losing some money and finding some alcohol. Or it was one guy losing some alcohol and finding some money. Whichever way you want to look at it.

If it was a face-to-face meeting, the moonshiner would place the liquor on a table, and the customer would place the money on a chair. After a short conversation, the customer would take the alcohol and the moonshiner would take the money and leave.

Pretty smart, right?

Wrong.

It was still a crime.

The Great Tulsa Liquor Conspiracy

In early 1957, a liquor conspiracy investigation rocked the Tulsa area, and the Tulsa Police Commissioner, the Tulsa Police Chief, and a journalist that was well-versed in the illegal liquor racket were among 20 people indicted on allegations of conspiracy to violate U.S. liquor laws.

Police commissioner Jay L. Jones, police chief Paul J. Livingston, and Tulsa Tribune reporter Nolen Bulloch were among the men, and women, indicted by a federal grand jury Thursday, February 21, 1957 on charges of violating federal liquor laws, involving pay offs.

It was basically a police protection payoff racket for illegal booze, gambling, and prostitution.

Bulloch was the reporter that gave Cleo Epps the name "The Queen of the Bootleggers" and was basically the beat reporter for illegal liquor sales, writing numerous exposes on the alcohol-related crimes.

After hearing about the indictment, Tribune Managing Editor Harmon Phillips released this statement about Bulloch: "We had noted the probable trend of the grand jury several weeks ago. At that time, we discussed the entire matter with Mr. Bulloch and made an independent inquiry. We have complete confidence in his integrity."

Six police officers, six bootleggers, bail bondsmen, and bar operators were also indicted.

The Tulsa World newspaper claims a reliable source said the estimated payoffs totaled $25,000 a month or higher. Police Chief Livingston was immediately suspended along with any officer named in the indictment.

Thirty overt acts were listed, including the disbursement of pay offs for several high-ranking officials. It was alleged that in April of 1956, at the home of Charles Hirrlinger, near Turley, police commissioner Jay Jones, police chief Paul Livingston, Jack Gott, John E, McAfee, bootlegger John Bill Edwards (Tommy Martin Edwards' brother), Tribune reporter Nolen Bulloch, and Hirrlinger determined the distribution of payments, after expenses, of course, to be received from gamblers, bootleggers, and prostitutes and be divided as follows: Jones 40 percent, Livingston 20 percent, Gott 20 percent, Bulloch 10, and the remaining 10 percent to be divided equally between McAfee, Edwards and Hirrlinger.

It was also alleged that Bulloch met with Cleo Epps at Bill's Truck Stop just east of Tulsa on State Highway 33 during the summer of 1953, and that Bulloch met with bootlegger Archie Moore, James F. O'Brien, and former chief of detectives Harold Haus in September of 1953.

Some of the allegations were that certain officers were promoted or demoted according to how they treated certain bootleggers, pimps, and gamblers.

The grand jury panel, made up of 21 people, investigated federal violations, hearing from 130 different witnesses that testified about events that occurred from January 1, 1948 to February 21, 1957.

On Friday, March 15, the grand jury added Cleo Epps' name to the list of the indicted and she testified that bootleggers and gamblers chipped in to pay Nolen Bulloch to avoid unfavorable publicity about their activities. She said she paid the Tribune reporter for around four months in 1948, then stopped the payments for five months, and started back up again.

Epps said Bulloch came to Bill's Truck Stop, a cafe and gas station she operated, and told her she needed to pay $2,000 a month or Bulloch would "close me up."

Bulloch told Epps he would padlock the truck stop if she didn't pay up, and he was right. A short time later, Epps showed up at the truck stop and there was a padlock on the door after liquor was found in a car parked outside of the building.

She started paying Bulloch, again.

Several witnesses testified they paid money to Epps to pay off Bulloch, and Epps said she did not receive any negative press from Bulloch while she was paying monthly.

However, three of the 20 indicted got lucky. Tribune reporter Nolen Bulloch, bootlegger Bernard Williams, and Bondsman Clifford E. Wells walked out of the courtroom free men on Wednesday, April 24, 1957. Judge Royce H. Savage ruled that the government had not met the burden of proof to establish a link between the three men and the alleged police protection payoff racket. Technically, the three men were acquitted by the judge.

Now, there were 17 co-defendants instead of 20, but the three men didn't leave empty-handed. They were served with witness subpoenas as they walked out of the courtroom. They had turned from defendants to witnesses.

Judge Savage said of the acquittals: "In the first place, the government had made observations of a rather general character. Evidence presented by the government in this case is not sufficient to go to the jury on the question of whether the defendants, or any of them, entered into an unlawful conspiracy as charged on or about the year 1948.

"My view is that all conspiracies going back to 1948 has not been established. You should have in mind that in May 1947, a change in the laws of Oklahoma was made with respect to the transportation and importation of whiskey into the state."

As far as payments were concerned, Savage said there was not sufficient evidence to prove any sort of conspiracy.

Of the 17 defendants, 16 were found guilty for conspiracy to import liquor into Oklahoma. Theopolis Scoggins, a black grocer, was acquitted.

CHAPTER SEVEN
Lost and Found

The day after Cleo Epps' disappearance, no one was looking for her because no one knew she was missing.

On Thursday, November 13, 1970, Carol Horsey walked out to a pasture to feed the horses that grazed there. The pasture was less than a mile west of Union Avenue and south of 61st Street. As she was walking toward the horses, Horsey noticed something on the ground and knelt down to touch the reddish liquid substance.

It was a little after 3 p.m., and the sun was still shining bright. She reached down and dabbed some of it on her finger and knew what it was immediately. To Horsey, it was obvious she had just rubbed blood between her thumb, index and middle fingers. Rubbing the liquid in a circle, it was still sticky and wet and smelled like rusty iron.

The blood was as thick as ketchup but was much darker in color, and some of it on the ground was starting to turn black. Her eyes went from her fingers down to the pool of blood and back to her fingers several times. On the ground, there was enough blood to deduce something bad had happened there recently.

It wasn't fresh, but it wasn't dried either. She thought to herself that it couldn't have been there but a day or two, and it might be human.

She called the Tulsa Police Department to make a report, and the dispatcher said they would send out a unit. An officer arrived at the pasture several hours later, and it had gotten dark outside. In Oklahoma, it can get dark around 6 p.m. due to Daylight Savings Time, where everyone sets their clocks back an hour in the fall. In the dark, the officer looked down at the pool of blood and said it was more than likely from an animal, such as a deer that had been skinned by a hunter.

No blood samples were taken by the officer, but Horsey scraped up a bit of the blood into a glass bottle and put it in her refrigerator. She couldn't help but think it might be linked to a crime, but she threw the bottle out several months later.

Two days after she found the blood, Horsey went back to the pasture and found two spent .22 caliber shell casings. After looking around the property, she found more blood on several feed troughs and tree stumps not too far from the original pool of blood.

She looked around for animal entrails, or a deer head that had been discarded by a disrespectful hunter but didn't find any. She also checked the horses for injury, but they were healthy and injury-free.

At that point, Horsey had done all she could do. She left the blood on the feed troughs and threw the shell casing in a trash pit.

Around three months later, Horsey called the police again to report what she had found, but, this time, they were more interested in what she had to say.

*****

On Friday, November 20, 1970, the pick-up truck owned by Cleo Epps was found in the parking lot of Union Square Shopping Center, right where she left it when she went to meet Albert McDonald and Tom Lester Pugh only eight days before.

The truck, located at 51st and Union Avenue in West Tulsa, was hard to miss, but it still took a few days to figure out that Epps was missing. In the past, she would leave for a few days to bring back a truckload of whiskey, but the whiskey business had slowed down, and the 61-year old former bootlegger kept more of a routine schedule. As a matter of fact, she was known for her routine.

Now that most of her business ventures were mostly legal, Epps was living a life of regular patterns and had an impressive talent for being on time. The departure of that regular routine could only mean something was very wrong. However, since she wasn't completely legal in her business dealings, calling the police immediately wasn't necessarily an option until family and friends could figure out what was really going on or where she had gone.

Epps also spent long hours on her land, clearing brush and using dynamite to blow up stumps in order to pave the way for new houses, but she would always show up to the Bough's house for dinner. The Boughs had now eaten by themselves without any word from Epps for eight days.

That Friday, police were called immediately, and they started with the preliminary testing of the truck but did not find any blood or fingerprints. There weren't any signs of a struggle and nothing seemed to be out of the ordinary other than the owner of the vehicle, Cleo Epps, was missing.

Her purse, with her pocketbook and a bottle of medication, was in plain sight in the cab of the truck and nothing was missing.

That night, District Attorney S.M. Buddy Fallis received a phone call from a Tulsa police officer who said, "Buddy, we found Cleo's pickup."

Unfortunately for Epps' family and friends, the discovery of her truck did not lead to her whereabouts. Each day that passed was agonizing for the people that loved her, and they would have to wait even longer.

The Tulsa Newspapers didn't pick up on the missing woman until after her truck was found on Friday. The Tulsa World published a story in the Tuesday, November 24, 1970 edition about her disappearance and the discovery of the abandoned truck.

Epps' nephew Tommy Gilbert Jr. never gave up looking for his beloved aunt, and he searched anytime he could.

Late November turned into December and December turned into January. It was getting colder and colder, and, in Oklahoma, December through February is generally the coldest time of the year.

On February 24, 1971, Tommy Gilbert was, again, looking for his aunt. He found one of her shoes near an abandoned farmhouse, located near 6500 S. Union in West Tulsa, only a short distance from where her truck was found. He called his father, Tom Gilbert Sr., Epps' younger brother, and he arrived at the property. They recognized the shoe as one Epps would wear to work in, and they started looking around the house for more items that might belong to her.

It's been reported that the Gilberts offered a reward for the discovery of Cleo Epps' body, and they received tips, starting around the day her truck was found.

Amateur sleuths would show up at the Gilbert's house or call day and night with tips on where they thought the female bootlegger would be found.

A well-known criminal from Sapulpa was constantly giving the Gilberts tips, but most of them didn't bear fruit. Some people have said he kept giving them false hopes until the reward money was to his liking, and he eventually gave them the correct information -- some people say.

A psychic medium, or fortune teller, from Dallas, Texas called the Gilberts and told them to look for a shoe and a Miller Beer sign. It wasn't much to go on, but it was something.

Tom Gilbert Sr., Tommy's father, eventually got a hold of Tulsa Police Chief Jack Purdie and told him to go to the southwest Tulsa supermarket where the truck was found, and the chief, and a caravan of black and white cars, converged on the Warehouse Market Grocery Store parking lot. The Gilberts met them there, and the caravan then headed to the dilapidated home. Around 50 police cars trickled in from Tulsa, Sapulpa, and Creek County, and the bevy of officers spread out and searched all around the house, but it was obvious where Epps would be if she was there.

Chief Purdie left the parking lot and glanced at the now empty spot. The last time anyone had seen Cleo Epps alive she was getting out of her vehicle and into another. He started down Union Avenue again and eventually turned onto a dirt road that led right to the house that Tom Gilbert and his son were standing near. They had already gotten out of their vehicle and were waiting on Chief Purdie. The chief stopped his car in front of the house, but the dirt road kept going around to the back, and that's where the Gilbert men told Purdie they had found something.

First, they took Purdie to the spot where Tommy Gilbert had found a shoe, and then they headed for the water cistern on the side of the house.

The house was made of wood, brick and stone and no one had lived in the dwelling for many years. The large farmhouse had several rooms and wasn't your typical-sized home a farmer would build.

The house ironically belonged to an old bootlegger that produced and distributed moonshine out of the house. It was also once a tavern or speakeasy where men would come to unwind after a long day of work. But those days were over, and the house had seen better days.

Tommy Gilbert poked his head inside the door of the house and immediately saw a dead coyote that got trapped in the house and either starved or froze to death. Holding the shoe he found, Tommy looked around the room and saw several beer signs, including a Miller Beer sign.

The psychic told the family to look for a shoe and a Miller Beer sign. She was 2-for-2.

The multi-room house was built with brown and tan sandstone bricks in various shapes and sizes held together with mortar. It had numerous windows, and a tall chimney. The front of the house had a rather large square hole as if someone attempted to make a garage. It also could have been a large window. Above that hole, stone and wooden two-by-fours were falling down, causing the bricks to fall off of the barely-standing house.

It appeared to have been victim to a fire at one point, and the house was obviously uninhabitable.

On the side was a water cistern located down in the ground. The cistern had a brick enclosure above it, and it had a small lid for access. However, by 1971, most of the brick was gone, exposing a large hole with broken stone and cement around it.

The lid was still there and was cemented to some of the brick around it, as if someone tried to close off the hole years ago.

The cistern was around six-feet deep.

As the men walked towards the house, Tom Gilbert repeated the story he had just told the chief when they were on the phone only minutes earlier. He told Purdie that he looked down in the hole and had trouble seeing so he grabbed a long piece of wire and started poking around. He hit something "soft" and left the property to phone Purdie.

The property was a 39-acre piece of land owned by the estate of Harry S. Boyd, who was a Tulsa businessman and investor. Boyd had made the final payment on the land on November 12, 1963 – five years to the day that Cleo Epps went missing. Boyd had purchased the property from Clarence W. Pate.

The crunch of the dead grass under their feet was loud, a bit louder due to the cold air and lack of houses or buildings around, and the harsh wind occasionally produced a low creepy whistle as it whipped around the trees and the structures.

There were three abandoned adobe-type houses spread out on the property with a thick wooded area behind them. A gate was built around the property and wooden materials and some of the roof was intentionally removed to deter people from squatting in the abandoned houses, but it was obviously to no avail.

With some snow still on the ground from a snowstorm the previous Sunday, the men noticed the footprints and markings of animals that had been around the cistern. It appeared the animals were walking around, trying to find a way to get to what they smelled.

The smell hit the men immediately. It was pungent and had a musty overpowering stench that could only be described as the smell of death.

Purdie looked down the hole and saw what looked like a piece of fleshy tissue floating in the water and ordered officers and everyone else to get back. However, they needed to find a way to get down there.

Workers from the City of Tulsa were called and told to bring a truck with a pump so they could drain the cistern, but, first, they had to use a truck to remove the lid before they could do anything.

With the help of the Tulsa Fire Department, the workers pumped some of the water out of the hole and more pieces of fleshy tissue spit out of the pump with the foul brown water.

Now, someone had to go down there.

That job went to Tulsa County Identification Sgt. Tom Lewallen, and he was familiar with getting his hands dirty, literally. Sgt. Lewallen rolled up his sleeves and crawled down through the two-foot square opening. He had to take a deep breath for two reasons: he needed to make his chest as small as possible to get through the hole, and he wanted to hold his breath for as long as he could before inhaling what was down in the hole.

Lewallen had to gather any and all physical evidence and supervise the removal of the body. There was a body down there, but it was covered with rocks.

When he got down into the hole, he saw a woman. She was lying in a 2-foot by 6-foot tank and covered with rocks. She was also partially submerged in water.

Police had now found what they had been searching for since November 20, three months prior. They found the body of Cleo Epps. However, she had been missing since November 12, but they didn't know it at the time.

Members of the press started to arrive at the scene, and they were allowed to get near the house and take pictures while the body was still underground. Photographers from the Tulsa World, Tulsa Tribune and Sapulpa Herald were walking around taking pictures, asking officers questions as the flash bulbs of their cameras constantly went off. However, when the body was to be lifted from the cistern, the news media had to clear the area and couldn't take pictures of the extraction.

Journalists were also there asking questions, but Purdie wasn't answering them. He still didn't know anything.

The bootleg queen had been carelessly crammed through the two-foot square at the opening of cistern, and rocks of all sizes were thrown in on top of her.

Before investigators could drain part of the tank, they had to remove several hundred pounds of rock that covered Epps' partially decomposing body. It was trapped under the rocks and part of her was in four feet of water.

It was now time for Lewallen to go to work.

While he was down in the tank, numerous officers walked up to the hole and looked down, but when the deadly odor hit their nostrils they would immediately back up, gagging and plugging their noses.

Lewallen was down in the hole for over two-hours and some of that time was spent removing the rocks from on top of the Epps' body. He lifted nearly 40 rocks from softball-sized to the size of a package of roofing shingles. The biggest weighed well over 100 pounds.

The task was not for the weak, squeamish, or faint of heart.

Because the smell was too much to handle for a beat cop, some of the officers took turns grabbing the rocks from Lewallen, taking smell breaks.

Lewallen was a handsome man in his 30s with thick brown hair, and he was physically fit. He had to be in order to have the stamina to do his job properly.

He ordered the workers to leave some of the water in the tank because he didn't want any evidence to be lost. He had to do his job, which was already difficult, while wading in what can only be described as "sewage."

It wasn't the worst Lewallen has dealt with in his career, but it was still bad.

When the rocks had been finally removed, he had to take measurements and photographs and make a detailed examination of everything he saw down there.

When all of that was completed, Lewallen supervised the removal of Epps' partially decomposing body. She was carefully placed in a black canvas body bag that had four strap-like handles, two at the top of the bag and two at the bottom. Four men grabbed one strap each and carried Epps to a truck that was waiting to take her for an autopsy.

Before she was placed in the bag, Tom Gilbert made an official "identification."

With a sorrowful look on his face, he glanced at Chief Purdie and said, "That's Cleo Epps."

Epps was identified from the rings on her fingers, a sweater, keys to the truck, and the matching shoe whose mate led to the discovery of her body.

If it were a robbery gone bad, the expensive rings would be gone, and Epps' purse and truck would have been taken, as well. This was a murder for hire or revenge.

The Boughs also made an identification. The shoe Tommy Gilbert found was taken to the Bough's house. They told officers it was the shoe Epps wore to work on her houses, and they identified the paint on the shoe as the same paint they used on the day she went missing.

Lewallen noticed something strange when the body was being lifted out of the hole. Epps' head was covered. A towel had been wrapped around her head and there were two holes in the towel, both were a quarter-inch in diameter. More than likely, the towel preserved some evidence.

There was no doubt she had been murdered.

Chief Purdie made an interesting statement to the press that was printed in the Tulsa World the following day.

Talking about Tom Gilbert, Purdie said, "He told me an informant told him where to look."

For some, it seemed improbable that the Gilbert men would have stumbled upon Epps' remains after fruitlessly searching that area over and over for three months.

Within 24 hours, an autopsy was performed in the garage of Moore Funeral Home on Peoria Avenue in

Tulsa. Due to the condition of Epps' body and the smell of the corpse, Medical Examiner Robert Fogel chose the funeral home's garage as the site of the autopsy.

The examination was just a formality.

After the autopsy, it was determined Epps' death was a homicide and was the result of two bullets to the head. Eventually, ballistic tests identified the bullets as coming from a .22 caliber firearm, the same caliber of weapon Pugh was known to carry.

The two bullets were still lodged in her skull.

However, the medical examiner also discovered that she was suffering from cancer, lymphoma, and she probably had only three or four months to live if she hadn't been murdered. Cleo Epps was dying of cancer.

The Tulsa World published a story about the missing woman's body being found in the Thursday, February 25, 1971 edition. The story was accompanied by a picture of the hole Cleo Epps was found in. It was taken by World photographer Stephen Crane.

Cleo Epps' body found with bullet in head

By Nick Stuart
Of the World Staff

The decomposed body of the long-time state "bootleg queen" Mrs. Cleo Epps, with a bullet lodged in the head, was found in a septic tank on an isolated southwest Tulsa farm Wednesday afternoon.

"There is no question she was murdered," Tulsa Police Chief Jack Purdie said Wednesday night after an autopsy was performed.

"She had been shot in the head before her body was put in the septic tank," he said.

The body was found by a relative of Mrs. Epps, who said an informer had told him where to look.

NO MARKS of a violent death were visible when the body was removed from the septic tank.

Mrs. Epps had been the object of a two-county search since November 12 when she disappeared, and her abandoned pickup truck was found on a parking lot just over a mile from the spot where her body was found Wednesday.

She vanished three weeks after appearing before a Tulsa County grand jury probing the bombing of District Judge Fred Nelson's car.

Her body was found as a second Tulsa County grand jury probed the bombings, including the explosion Sunday which destroyed the In Court Tavern in Tulsa.

Purdie said Tom Gilbert, brother of 60-year old, Sapulpa area woman, called him Wednesday and asked the chief to meet him at 51st Street and Union Avenue.

Purdie said he met Gilbert and followed the Wagoner County rancher to the deserted farm near 65th Street and Union Avenue.

"He told me an informant had told him where to look," Purdie said.

The chief said Gilbert and son, Tommy Gilbert Jr. had been searching the farm since getting the tip and earlier found a shoe he believed belonged to Mrs. Epps.

THE SHOE was taken to the home near Tulsa of the last person known to have seen Mrs. Epps alive, Billie Popovich.

She said a spot of paint on the shoe was identical to the kind of paint Mrs. Epps had been using in her Creek County housing development the day of her disappearance.

Purdie said, after finding the shoe, Gilbert uncovered the septic tank and poked around inside with a piece of wire.

"He said he hit something soft and called me," Purdie said.

Police used a pickup truck to pull part of the cover off the two-section tank.

The tank was filled with water, probably from last Sunday's snow.

TULSA STREET and water department personnel were called and drained the 3 feet of water from the tank.

Purdie said there were pieces of apparent human tissue floating in the water.

Police Sgt. Tom Lewallen climbed into the narrow-left chamber of the tank and removed about three feet of rock, uncovering the body.

Police said the body had apparently been pushed into the tank through a 2-foot square opening at the top, then the rock had been dumped in.

THE BODY lying on its side, was lifted from the well after Tommy Gilbert had identified the remains as that of Mrs. Epps.

Police said preliminary identification was made from rings found the dead woman's fingers and from a sweater, keys and the shoes found at the scene.

"The body is that of Cleo Epps," Gilbert said.

The body was found near one of three adobe-type buildings on the farm.

A dirt road led from Union Avenue to the rear property and runs by the ramshackle house near where the body was found.

Police would not comment Wednesday when asked if Mrs. Epps was slain at the scene or killed elsewhere and her body brought to the deserted farm.

ABOUT 50 LAW enforcement officials converged on the farm and cordoned off an area within a 100-yard radius of the septic tank while hunting for clues.

No one, except lawmen, was admitted within the area for over two hours. Newsmen were allowed to enter the area just before the body was removed from the tank.

Mrs. Epps was known as "Queen of the Bootleggers" during prohibition days in Oklahoma. She was convicted in federal court in 1966, won a reversal but later lost the reversal on a ruling by the 10th Circuit Court of Appeals.

She remained free after conviction awaiting appeal.

She had been indicted in a moonshine operation which allegedly poured an estimated 2,000 gallons of illegal whiskey a month into the Tulsa area.

ON THE DAY she was last seen, Mrs. Epps had spent the day painting one of numerous rental houses she owned in the area northeast of Sapulpa.

After returning to her home between Tulsa and Sapulpa, she drove her pickup truck to the home of a neighbor where she ate.

Gilbert said that after dinner, an acquaintance of Mrs. Epps came to the house and asked to talk to her. The acquaintance and Mrs. Epps left the neighbor's house in separate vehicles.

She then went to the home of another acquaintance and there had two telephone conversations.

AFTER THE second one, she said she was going to meet someone in the parking lot of a supermarket and would return shortly. She was clad in green slacks and a white sweater.

She was not seen after that and it was 10 days before her truck was found parked near the supermarket. Inside was a bag containing personal belongings and medicine.

Mrs. Epps owned several pieces of property in four counties. She also held mortgages on an east Tulsa motel and several businesses in Creek and Tulsa counties.

Withdrawals had been made from her bank account after November 5, according to a relative.

Another article was written for the B-section of the same Tulsa World edition that would delve into Epps' state of mind in the last few months of her life and why she was constantly looking over her shoulder.

Last Days Weary, Say Friends of Cleo Epps

By Jim Henderson
Of the World Staff

In the last days before she disappeared, it is told, Cleo Epps had grown weary and perhaps a bit frightened. Among her friends were gamblers, bootleggers, burglars and fences in eastern Oklahoma and word was leaking out that Cleo, of all people, was a police informant.

In the weeks leading up to the evening of November 12, 1970, the last night that Cleo Epps was seen alive, the police had never had a greater need of an informant.

Someone had tried to assassinate a Tulsa District Court judge, and someone had murdered wealthy Osage County rancher E.C. Mullendore and someone thought Cleo Epps might know something about both crimes.

IN OCTOBER, Tulsa County grand jury was seated to investigate the bombing of a care that nearly killed Judge Fred Nelson. Sometime during the week-long probe, a short heavy woman wearing a long coat and red wig was hurried in and out of the grand jury room.

The disguise apparently was a ploy to protect Cleo Epps, who had been known as "queen of the bootleggers" before repeal of prohibition, but oldtimers who had witnessed her frequent appearances in court saw through the masquerade.

Word began circulating through the courthouse corridors; Cleo Epps had not only fingered the bomber but had told the grand jury who stole the dynamite, who buried it on a Creek County farm and who retrieved it and turned it over to the bomber.

If, indeed, that rumor was accurate, it could never be substantiated because of the secrecy of the grand jury proceedings.

BUT WHEN SHE disappeared on the night of November 12, law enforcement officials expressed little surprise. It was widely assumed that her probable death and her testimony to the grand jury were closely related.

But Cleo Epps apparently was not a woman of limited knowledge where the eastern Oklahoma underworld is concerned. If she had knowledge of the Nelson bombing, it is just as likely she had other information of other crimes.

Not long before she disappeared, Mrs. Epps reportedly told a friend: "They're going to kill me about that Mullendore thing. I wish they would leave me out of it."

She has been the subject of frequent conversation during the current grand jury investigation into crime in Tulsa County and many of the witnesses who have been subpoenaed knew her well.

ONE OF THEM is Albert McDonald, a 45-year old former Collinsville man who has been a key figure in the bombing probes. His lawyer, in fact, has conceded that "it is common knowledge they are trying to link Al to the Nelson bombing."

McDonald and Mrs. Epps had been close friends for many years and he often described her as "a fine person... who wouldn't hurt anybody."

He has disputed claims that she was a police informant and although the grand jury had questioned him about her disappearance, McDonald maintains that they were friends.

He was one of the last persons to see her the night she left a neighbor's home, drove to a shopping center parking lot at 51st Street and Union Avenue and disappeared. Her pickup was found there about 10 days later.

OFFICERS ALSO were not surprised Wednesday when a body hauled from a well about a mile from the parking lot was identified as Cleo Epps.

"Anybody who would kill Cleo would have to be crazy," a grand jury witness said after the body was identified. "She had a heart as big as Texas."

A one-time schoolteacher and wife of a Tulsa lawyer, Mrs. Epps was introduced to bootlegging by her second husband, who made his living in illegal whiskey. When that marriage soured, she started her own business and eventually controlled the wholesale and retail traffic in a number of eastern Oklahoma counties.

She apparently invested her bootlegging earnings wisely and when she died at the age of 60, held property reported to be worth nearly half a million dollars.

HER BODY WAS discovered Wednesday after her family received information from an "informant." It also came at the peak of the Tulsa County grand jury investigations into eastern Oklahoma bombings.

Some law enforcement officials hinted that the juxtaposition of the discovery of Cleo Epps and the grand jury probe is more than coincidental.

Earlier this week, the In Court Lounge, across the street from the courthouse was bombed and the proprietor theorized that I was because grand jury witnesses had been "hanging around" there.

"Someone," a courthouse source said, "is trying to make a point."

The article mentions the Mullendore murder several times, but Epps was never linked to that crime.

Eugene Claremont "E.C." Mullendore III was a wealthy 33-year old rancher in Osage County, living on his 130,000-acre family-ranch called the Cross Bell Ranch.

Osage County is the largest and oldest county in Oklahoma. It's located in the northeastern part of Oklahoma and Pawhuska is the county seat and largest city. The county also has parts of Tulsa, Bartlesville, Sand Springs, Skiatook, and Ponca City. It has around 2,300 square miles of land.

E.C. Mullendore III's father Gene Mullendore Jr. owned the ranch and handed the ranch operations over to his son, E.C., in 1960 due to Gene's failing health. E.C. reportedly ran up over $10 million in debts due to his family's lavish lifestyle.

On September 26, 1970, E.C. was beaten and shot between the eyes in the den of the Cross Bell Ranch in an apparent burglary gone bad.

E.C.'s bodyguard and assistant Damon "Chub" Anderson claimed to be upstairs running a bath when he heard the gunshot. He ran down stars, was shot in the shoulder, and returned fire on two assailants fleeing from the home.

No one was ever charged with E.C.'s murder, but, 40 years later, Anderson allegedly admitted that, along with his brother-in-law, the two killed E.C. and staged the break-in to look like a robbery, including Anderson's gunshot wound. Anderson died later that year in 2010.

*****

The funeral for Cleo Epps, The Queen of the Bootleggers, was held Saturday afternoon, February 27, 1971 at Owen Funeral Home in Sapulpa, Oklahoma, and she was laid to rest at Greenhill Cemetery in Sapulpa. She was survived by her foster son, Richard Carl Main, and two brothers, Tom Gilbert of Wagoner, Oklahoma, and Samuel Gilbert, of Magazine, Ark.

Among the 150 people who attended her funeral were criminals, senators, law enforcement agents, judges, lawyers, friends, family, and city officials, such as, U.S. Representative Ed Edmondson, State senator Edward Collins, from Sapulpa, and District Court Judge Bill Heyworth of Muskogee.

Edmondson attended the funeral to support Epps' brother Tom Gilbert who was his Wagoner County campaign chairman.

Epps was a soft-spoken, compassionate, generous soul who went to great lengths to help people. She just happened to be one of the most notorious bootleggers in the area's history.

She was liked everywhere she went.

Greenhill cemetery is located southeast of Sapulpa just off of Teel road headed out of town towards Kiefer, Oklahoma. Greenhill cemetery started in 1962 and was still considered relatively new when Epps was buried in 1971. She was laid to rest in the same cemetery as her mother who died just four years before in 1966.

Sarah Daisy (Groh) Gilbert died in 1966 at the age of 76. Her grave marker is nearly identical to her daughter Cleo Epps' marker. The 1-foot by 2-foot bronze plaque is the same but without the grey marble slab. It's a bronze rectangular plate with roses adorned on each side and a small bronze flower vase at the top, it reads: "MOTHER Daisy Gilbert 1889-1966."

In an odd twist, the Sunday, May 23, 1971 edition of the Daily Oklahoman, announced that Cleo Epps was named executrix of her dear friend Billie Popovich's estate. It was around six months after Epps' murder. The will was dated September 30, 1969, over a year before Epps' death, but it insinuated Epps' had debts and obligations to Popovich. However, they were absolved upon Popovich's death.

It was more than likely legal jargon, and it's been rumored that Popovich and Epps both owned an interest in the Avalon Steakhouse at one time.

Cleo Named Executrix

SAPULPA – The will of a Sapulpa woman who died a week ago named as executrix of $100,000 estate an old friend and police character who was murder several months ago.

According to the will of Mrs. Billie Popavitch (sp) who died Saturday (May 22, 1971) at the age of 71, slain bootleg queen Cleo Epps is executrix of the estate.

The will dated September 30, 1969, also said, "As consideration for the loyalty and lifelong friendship of Cleo Epps, I hereby forgive and release all debts and obligations owed me by said Cleo Epps at the time of my death."

CHAPTER EIGHT
Crime and The Great Depression

The phrase, "Necessity is the mother of all invention" means when the need for something becomes imperative, one is forced to find creative ways to achieve it.

The same can be said of the great depression and crime. Sometimes, a person had to do what they had to do to make a buck, and that included robbing, stealing, and killing. A lot of times, they did it just to put food on the table.

Some criminals crossed the line as a necessity and immediately realized they liked it.

Ask anyone that knew Cleo Epps and they will tell you that she became a bootlegger out of necessity, and it was clear that she was very good at it.

Epps got into bootlegging during The Great Depression.

She left Arkansas in the 1920s during the boll weevil infestation that played a big role in the depression. The boll weevil is a beetle that feeds on cotton crops, destroying everything in sight. The beetle came to the United States from Mexico and infested all cotton-growing areas in the U.S. by the 1920s.

The Mexican Boll Weevil infestation started in the 1890s and ended in the early 1920s, but the devastation was felt for years to come.

Epps and her family felt the sting of the beetle raid, and Epps, and some of her family, left for Oklahoma, looking for a better life.

The Great Depression affected the south greatly, and Oklahoma was not spared. The one-two punch of the Dust Bowl and The Great Depression nearly crippled the state with drought, high winds, and dust, forcing thousands of Oklahoma families to head west to California to find work and escape what could only be described as "hell on earth" at the time.

The Dust Bowl, which was caused from severe drought, wind erosion, high winds, and the lack of agricultural knowledge, hit in the early 1930s while the country was already suffering from a depression.

The Great Depression was the worst economic collapse in the history of the United States, starting with the stock market crash of 1929, and it lasted around 10 years.

The Dust Bowl and The Great Depression partnered together, forcing normal people to do things they wouldn't normally do to feed their families. The crimes committed during that time also led to the validation of the Federal Bureau of Investigation.

Oklahoma is no stranger to crime, especially as a result of The Great Depression, and some infamous criminals were either born in Oklahoma, made Oklahoma their home, or spent some time in the Sooner State while running from the law.

George "Machine Gun Kelly" Barnes

George "Machine Gun Kelly" Barnes, like Cleo Epps, was a bootlegger and businessman. However, he went a little further with his criminal enterprises than Epps ever did.

He was born George Kelly Barnes on July 18, 1895 in Memphis Tennessee, and got his nickname from his favorite weapon, a Thompson submachine gun, given to him by his wife Kathryn.

His wife, Kathryn Barnes, was born Cleo Mae Brooks on March 18, 1904 in Rockwall, Texas. Her original name was "Cleo," and, for years, it was rumored that she was named after Cleo Epps, the infamous bootlegger. However, Kathryn Barnes was born five years before Epps, and Epps' reputation was clean until around the 1940s.

It's still a great rumor.

Kathryn Barnes changed her name from Cleo when she was around 15 years old, the same year she married her first husband and had a child.

She was married three times before settling down with Machine Gun Kelly, if it could be called "settling down." Her third husband was also a bootlegger.

Kathryn was already a criminal by the time she married Machine Gun Kelly, her fourth husband, and they started a life of crime together, including one of the most notorious kidnappings in Oklahoma history. The crime would also be the end of their criminal endeavors.

Just barely an adult, Machine Gun Kelly started bootlegging and committing minor burglaries and robberies.

He left Tennessee and headed west because he had a lot of heat on him. In 1928, he was arrested in Tulsa, Oklahoma for smuggling liquor onto an Indian Reservation. He was released early from his three-year sentence at Leavenworth Penitentiary in Kansas, and, in 1933, pulled off the successful kidnapping of Oklahoma City oil tycoon Charles F. Urschel.

On July 22, 1933, Machine Gun Kelly and his associate Albert L. Bates interrupted a bridge card game at the Urschel home in Oklahoma City, and Urschel and fellow oilman, Walter Jarrett, were kidnapped at gunpoint.

After the two kidnappers figured out which victim was Urschel, they released Jarrett just outside of OKC.

Machine Gun Kelly asked for and was paid $200,000 in ransom money.

After being held at a farmhouse in Texas for just over a week, Urschel was released but was able to give FBI agents crucial details that led them to the gang

On October 12, 1933, Machine Gun Kelly and Kathryn were found guilty and sentenced to life imprisonment.

After serving time at Alcatraz prison, and again at Leavenworth, George "Machine Gun" Kelly died of an apparent heart attack on his 59th birthday.

Kathryn served 25 years and was released. She spent the rest of her years in Oklahoma City and died in 1985.

Charles "Pretty Boy" Floyd

It was just a blip on the criminal's rap sheet, but Charles "Pretty Boy" Floyd had a run in with Tulsa Police and managed to get away during several events that could only be called "comical."

Charles Arthur "Pretty Boy" Floyd was born February 3, 1904 and mainly committed bank robberies in the Midwest and southern states. He was born in Georgia, but his family moved to Oklahoma when he was still a schoolboy.

Floyd once lived in Oklahoma as an adult, reportedly so his son could attend Tulsa Public Schools, and he committed crimes in the Tulsa area.

In 1932, Floyd and accomplice George Birdwell shot and killed special state investigator, Erv Kelley, in a shootout on some farmland southwest of Bixby.

At one point, the Tulsa Police and Floyd, with Birdwell in tow, engaged in a good old-fashioned car chase through the streets of Tulsa. With bullets flying from both Floyd's car and the police cars, the Tulsa Police gave up after their only Thompson submachine gun ran out of bullets.

The next night, Floyd and Birdwell were cornered at Floyd's residence on East Young Street, sort of.

Tulsa police knew the two criminals were in the house and fired tear gas canisters into the home, ordering the men to surrender. The officers rushed into the house to find it empty. Floyd and Birdwell had simply walked out of the back door and sauntered away from the scene. Officers had forgotten to cover the back of the house.

In 1933, Floyd was reportedly involved in the "Kansas City Massacre," a gunfight where four law enforcement officers were killed. However, Floyd sent a postcard to the Kansas City Police where he denied involvement in the massacre, and there is still a debate as to whether he participated or not.

Floyd was killed by Federal agents a year later in 1934.

Bonnie and Clyde

Clyde Barrow and Bonnie Parker, the infamous "Bonnie and Clyde," are known all over the world, and Barrow killed his first law enforcement officer while in Oklahoma.

If Bonnie was the gasoline, Clyde was the match, and when the two got together they started fires all over the south.

Clyde Barrow was born March 24, 1909 in Ellis County Texas, and Bonnie Elizabeth Parker was born October 1, 1910 in Rowena, Texas.

The two criminals met in 1930 and were dead only four years later.

While Parker was visiting family in Texas, Barrow killed a police officer in Stringtown, Oklahoma. Barrow was drinking with friends in the parking lot at a country dance, when Sheriff C.G. Maxwell and his deputy, Eugene C. Moore, approached the men. Barrow shot both. He did not kill the sheriff, but he did kill the deputy.

It was the first lawman killed by the "Barrow Gang," and, in the end, the number would be around ten.

The gang was known for the robberies of small rural stores that sometimes involved murder. They also committed thefts, kidnappings, auto thefts, and bank robberies. They killed around 13 people, including lawmen and civilians, and became famous for being a young couple, in love and on the run.

The Barrow Gang also stole Browning Automatic Rifles from a National Guard Armory in Enid, Oklahoma, giving them more firepower than the Thompson machine guns the FBI agents used.

Barrow and Parker were ambushed and killed by law enforcement officers on a rural road in Louisiana on Wednesday, May 23, 1934, ending the tale of Bonnie and Clyde.

Their bodies were riddled with bullets after six law enforcement agents opened fire on the love bird's stolen 1934 Ford Deluxe Sedan in Bienville Parish, Louisiana. The officers emptied the magazines of their automatic rifles, pistols, and shotguns into the car. It's reported that they continued to shoot even after knowing the two were more than likely dead.

The Ford had around 150 bullet holes and the interior was stained with Bonnie and Clyde's blood. The official coroner's report said the couple was shot a total of 43 times, but researchers claim both bodies sustained around 50 shots each.

Kate "Ma" Barker

In the early 1920s, the Barker Gang can be traced to Oklahoma, and they even lived in Tulsa for a period of time.

Ma Barker was born on October 8, 1873 in Missouri and had four criminal sons, Herman Barker, Lloyd Barker, Arthur "Doc" Barker, and Fred Barker, committing robberies and kidnappings, mainly.

Herman was the oldest, born in 1893, followed by Lloyd in 1897, Arthur in 1899, and Fred in 1901.

The four Barkers were introduced to professional crime after joining the Central Park Gang in Tulsa.

Due, in part, to J. Edgar Hoover's description of Ma Barker, the woman was widely known as the matriarch of the Barker Gang. She was described as blood-thirsty, vicious, deadly, dangerous, and resourceful. However, researchers claim she was hardly a criminal mastermind and was often sent to the movies while her sons committed the crimes.

In 1935, Ma Barker and her son, Fred, were both killed in a shootout with FBI agents at a house in Lake Weir, Florida.

According to reports, Fred's body was riddled with bullets, and his mother died of a single gunshot wound. A Thompson submachine gun was lying between the two.

They are buried in Welch, Oklahoma, next to Herman Barker, who died in 1927.

Doc Barker was involved in the murder of a Tulsa night watchman, and the gang was suspected of killing one of their former attorney's J. Earl Smith, who was found dead at Indian Hills Country Club.

He was eventually convicted of murder and kidnapping and handed a life sentence to be served at Alcatraz in California. In 1939, Doc Barker attempted to escape Alcatraz prison with several fellow inmates but was fatally shot and killed by guards.

In 1949, Lloyd Barker was shot and killed by his wife while living in Colorado. He was previously a cook in the U.S. Army and received an honorable discharge.

*****

Cleo Epps obviously turned to a life of crime out of necessity just like Pretty Boy Floyd, Ma Barker, Bonnie and Clyde, and Machine Gun Kelly, but there is no evidence that Epps ever hurt anyone.

She made her money selling illegal booze and turned that money into a legitimate real estate business. Epps eventually became a businesswoman, owning a motel, numerous houses, and property. However, the motel often housed criminals on the run or on the mend, and the property often hid illegal liquor.

But Cleo Epps never killed anyone, and the majority of depression-era criminals left a sea of bodies in their wakes that included, local law enforcement officers, federal agents, and civilians.

CHAPTER NINE
Albert McDonald and Thomas Lester Pugh

Albert McDonald and Thomas Lester Pugh were members of a deadly cast of characters that terrorized Oklahoma and several surrounding states up through 1970. They were appropriately called, "The Dixie Mafia."

Whether separate or together, the deadly duo of Pugh and McDonald left a pile of dead bodies, charred buildings, mangled cars, hollowed-out taverns, children without fathers, children without mothers, and frustrated district attorneys and judges.

Albert McDonald was known as "Big Al" around the Tulsa and Sapulpa areas because he was taller than most of the criminals he ran around with, especially Pugh, but, after 1974, he was only known as "Inmate 88394" at the Oklahoma State Prison in McAlester, Oklahoma. Also known as "Big Mac." Big Mac now owned Big Al.

McDonald, from Dewey, Oklahoma was 6-foot-2 and weighed around 200 pounds. In his mid-40s, he was a bit round in his midsection, causing him to wear his pants high around his belly button. He had jet-black straight hair that was hard to tame. It often looked like he just got out of bed and headed out the door without even touching a comb.

McDonald was mean. There is no other way to put it. He was real mean. He had no compassion or respect for human life.

He was a murderer, a thief, a bomber, a criminal, a burglar, a sadist, and an all-around bad person all the way to his core. McDonald didn't just play the part of a criminal. He lived it.

He had a disdain for law enforcement, and if a district attorney tried to speak to him, he wouldn't answer. He made no bones about who he was and what he could do.

At one point, McDonald and Cleo Epps were supposed to get married, and her family wasn't happy about it. Nearly everyone in the Epps-Gilbert family hated McDonald and did not want Cleo Epps to even associate with him let alone marry him.

Her foster son, Richard Main, especially didn't like McDonald, and it led to an injury. Main could do anything with his hands, and Epps taught him how to build and frame houses. He was an impressive carpenter and eventually joined the Navy.

When he was a teenager, Main was helping Epps build a house, and he was on the roof. The two started arguing about McDonald and Main was so upset he accidentally fell off of the roof. He made a full recovery, but he also made his point.

McDonald would join the Gilberts for holidays occasionally, but he usually kept to himself. However, the family knew about his checkered past and present.

In criminal case CRF-73-33, McDonald was convicted of murder in Bryan County on Friday, May 10, 1974. He was appropriately given a life sentence.

He was born February 23, 1925 and was 49 years old when started severing his life sentence.

*****

Thomas Lester Pugh was often described as a baby-faced bandit. He was also referred to as a "cocky little thug."

Standing at only 5-foot-6, his partner in crime, Albert McDonald, towered over him. Pugh was eventually convicted of one murder, charged with two others, and suspected in another.

Born April 2, 1937, Pugh was from Glenpool, Oklahoma, and was well-liked and popular in town. He excelled in sports at Glenpool High School and married his high school sweetheart, Mary Jo, the homecoming queen.

Pugh got into bootlegging just out of high school, and it led to other criminal endeavors.

After Pugh and McDonald killed Epps and stuffed her body into the water cistern, the two needed to lie low for a while. They fled to Arizona, but laying low wasn't their style, and their crime spree continued.

In Arizona, on January 18, 1971, the two committed an armed robbery, and the victims were Joe and Gertrude LaFortune, the parents of Robert LaFortune, who was the mayor of Tulsa at the time. They entered the Tulsa couple's Arizona hotel room, wearing masks. They helped themselves to some very expensive jewelry while the LaFortunes were out at the time.

Pugh was arrested for the robbery and transported back to Tulsa.

On Thursday, October 19, 1972, a Tulsa jury convicted Pugh in the murder of a man who testified against him in the Nelson car bombing grand jury proceedings. The man was also set to testify against Pugh again in an Arkansas arson case. However, before Pugh could start serving his sentence for case No. CRF-71-2169, Pugh was sent to Arizona to start his serving his 25 to 30-year sentence for the robbery of the LaFortunes.

Pugh was acquitted in the death of a man who was shot five times and buried in a grave covered with lime near Sand Springs in Osage County.

However, the prison bars did not stop his criminal activity, and there weren't too many prisons that could hold him. Pugh was able to win the trust of guards and other inmates, escaping from two different correctional facilities.

In the Arizona prison, he was charged with plotting to murder several judges, and was transferred to prisons in Kentucky and Missouri.

He was first sent to a Missouri prison and was the alleged leader in a prison break and a plot to assassinate two Arizona Superior Court judges. In 1974, guards found two loaded guns in Pugh's cell, and he was stabbed five times during a fight. Two years later, he was then transferred to a Kentucky prison in Eddyville, Kentucky.

In the Kentucky prison, Pugh, and 25-year old inmate, Thomas Eugene Cawthon, successfully escaped on October 25, 1976. From his cell, Pugh was the alleged ringleader of a five-state prison drug ring where drugs were being smuggled into numerous prisons, including the Oklahoma State Penitentiary. The two men escaped in a prison work farm truck, hiding in two large crates.

Cawthon admitted to committing around twenty robberies while on the run with Pugh in Oklahoma, New Mexico, Texas, and Missouri, and they even talked about possibly killing Tulsa District Attorney S.M. Buddy Fallis.

In 1977, while on the lam, he robbed a couple from Irvin, Texas. On October26, Pugh and Cawthon were living in an apartment in Irving, Texas when the FBI found them.

Outside of the apartment, Pugh saw the FBI and ran several yards before he ran into a wall of more federal agents with their guns pointed at his head. Pugh tossed his gun to the ground, raised his hands, and fell to his knees. He knew the drill. He had been there before, numerous times.

Both Pugh and Cawthon surrendered peacefully and neither the FBI nor the criminals fired a single shot.

Pugh was then held in Dallas, Texas to see if prison officials would send him back to Arizona, Oklahoma or Kentucky.

Then, nine years later, he was almost a free man despite owing prison sentences in four states.

In 1986, Pugh had served nine years of his sentence of life-plus 10 years for robbing the couple when he was up for early parole due to good behavior. He was scheduled to go to a halfway house in El Paso,

Texas and no other agency was notified he was about to be released. The clerk had misread the records sent from Oklahoma which said Pugh had been "acquitted on all Oklahoma cases."

However, he still owed Oklahoma a life sentence for murder.

A representative of the Texas prisons said a mistake was made due to a clerical error. The requests to transfer Pugh into the custody of other prisons in other states were lost. Apparently, Tulsa County Sheriff Frank Thurman learned of Pugh's possible release, and phone calls were made.

Eventually, Pugh was sent to Big Mac in McAlester, Oklahoma, and lived there until the day he died. Pugh died Wednesday, December 20, 2006 in a Department of Corrections medical center where he was taken after an apparent heart attack. He was 69 years old.

*****

On June 5, 1978, Albert McDonald was scheduled to be tried for the 1970 car bombing of Dist. Judge Fred Nelson, but that case would never go to trial. However, most people believe McDonald and his associate, Tom Lester Pugh wired the bomb to Nelson's ignition switch and placed it under the car on the driver's side.

Sapulpa attorney Jack Sellers, who represented McDonald said he was never "convicted cleanly" at any of his trials, and there was no physical evidence to connect him to the car bombing. However, Sellers claimed McDonald's acquittal of a previous murder trial was fair and just.

At around 2:40 p.m., Thursday, April 13, 1978, McDonald's throat was slashed near the showers in F block at Big Mac. After some recreational time out in the yard, McDonald began fighting with two other convicted murderers, and it resulted in his stabbing death.

By the time guards arrived, McDonald was in a pool of blood, and his throat had been slashed. He also had several stab wounds to his chest.

At age 53, McDonald's hair had turned from black to gray, which now looked even lighter surrounded by own crimson blood that spread from his neck and pooled under his head and around his shoulders. McDonald's bloody ending closed the book on his long and deadly life of crime.

Two homemade knives were found near his body, and he was still clutching a pipe that he used to try and defend himself.

The two inmates were taken into custody. McDonald's death followed another stabbing incident, involving two other inmates and an apparent suicide on the same day. They were unrelated to McDonald's murder.

Both Pugh and McDonald were linked to the murders of Cleo Epps, Tommy Martin Edwards, Arlis Delbert Self, and the attempted murder of District Judge Fred S. Nelson.

With robberies, car bombings, more bombings, and just about any other crime you can think of, Pugh and McDonald weren't to be messed with or crossed and testifying against them was just plain deadly.

The murders of Epps, Martin, and Self were revenge killings for their testimony in grand jury proceedings, involving Judge Nelson's attempted murder with a car bomb.

Tulsa County was assembling a second grand jury for the judge's car bombing after the first proceeding, but some of the witnesses were now dead. No one was ever convicted in the assassination attempt of Judge Nelson.

Pugh and McDonald were both charged with the Nelson crime, but it never went to trial. They were also both charged in the murder of Epps.

CHAPTER TEN
Three Witnesses, Three Murders

In the attempted murder and car bombing of Tulsa District Judge Fred S. Nelson, Cleo Epps and Arlis Delbert Self both testified against Albert McDonald and Thomas Pugh in a grand jury proceeding. Self was witness to an Arkansas arson committed by Tom Lester Pugh and agreed to testify when the case went to trial.

All three were found murdered.

Tommy Martin Edwards

On July 15, 1971 Tommy Martin Edwards told his wife he would be gone for a few days and left his trailer in the trailer park off of Riverside Drive in Tulsa.

After receiving a call from Edwards' wife in September, Tulsa Police began investigating her husband's disappearance. They drove out to Edwards' mailbox at his trailer, and there was mail stuffed in the mailbox and on the ground below it. Obviously, Edwards hadn't been there in a while.

On Tuesday, September 28, 1971, an anonymous call came into the Tulsa World News desk and asked, "Do you want to know where Martin Edwards is?"

The caller then gave directions to the grave that marked with a piece of a cardboard box and other trash items. The grave was near a pond on property owned by the Sand Springs Home, an orphanage started by Sand Springs town founder, Charles Page. The land was six miles northwest of Sand Springs in Osage County.

The similarities between the crime scenes of Edwards and Epps were uncanny and couldn't be coincidental.

Edwards body was found in a shallow, lime-soaked grave marked by a piece of cardboard, a can of antifreeze, a beer can, and several branches. He was shot five times in the head.

Edwards, a former bootlegger, was 51 years old when he was murdered and hadn't been convicted of a crime in over seven years, but he still associated with numerous criminals. The name Martin Edwards is nearly as synonymous with bootlegging whiskey in the 1930s, 1940s and 1950s as Cleo Epps, and he was not apologetic about his past.

Several hours after the first call to the Tulsa World, the caller phoned again and said, "Did you find the body?"

The body was found and taken to Moore Funeral home for an autopsy.

Dr. Robert Fogel performed an autopsy that night and said Edwards was shot three times in the back of the head and twice on the top of the head with a .38 caliber pistol. Fogel said the body was "extremely well preserved" due to a chemical reaction in the that turned it "into soap." There were no other violent signs to the body.

Lime had been dumped into the shallow grave and heavy rocks were placed over Edwards' body – just like Epps. Instead of destroying the body, the lime and heavy rains caused a chemical reaction. The soil around the body was constantly wet and the reaction turned the fat in Edwards' body to a soap-like substance, basically preserving the body, perfectly. It did the opposite of what the killers were hoping.

Edwards had just eaten a heavy meal and maybe even dined with his killers. There were no defensive wounds or signs of a struggle. Edwards had not resisted.

Edwards was found, but his 1968 green Plymouth was still missing. Tulsa Police did an aerial search of parts of Creek, Osage, and Tulsa Counties. The terrain was nearly impossible to trek by foot or vehicle, and the plane was the only other choice. The car was not found, and Edwards' shoes were also missing.

Since Edwards was found in Osage County, Thomas Lester Pugh was tried at the Osage County Courthouse in Pawhuska, Oklahoma, and his first trial ended in a mistrial because the jury saw Pugh coming out of an elevator in handcuffs and chains around his hands and ankles.

Pugh was again tried in June of 1972 for the murder of Edwards, and the state's case depended on the testimony of former friend and criminal, Rubie Charles "Bob" Jenkins who said Pugh and McDonald told him they killed Edwards and Self.

Pugh's attorney said Jenkins was promised he would go free if he testified against Pugh and that he had numerous criminal charges pending that would send him to prison for the rest of his life.

The state denied these allegations.

The defense paraded witnesses into the court to testify that Pugh didn't commit the murder of Edwards and named others that did. Clyde Morland pointed the finger at Jenkins and said Jenkins admitted to him that he killed Epps, Self and Edwards.

On Wednesday, June 28, 1971, the jury took just under an hour and 10 minutes to acquit Pugh of the murder of Tommy Martin Edwards.

Pugh looked at the jury and said, "God bless them all."

He later said, "If I get a fair trial in Tulsa as I did here, I'll be alright."

Pugh now awaited trials for the killing of Cleo Epps, Arlis Self, and the attempted murder of Judge Fred S. Nelson.

Arlis Delbert Self

Arlis Self knew he was on the "kill list" of McDonald and Pugh. He knew he was marked for death.

On Monday, March 30, 1971, McDonald and Pugh murdered Self for testifying against them in the grand jury proceedings for the Judge Nelson case. It wasn't the first murder, and it wouldn't be the last.

Self and his roommate, Beauford Nelson Bourland, were on a bender, drinking just about anything they could get their hands on. They bought a fifth of vodka, each drank a bit, and settled in for the night. Self and Bourland had drank all day and all night and drank some more before passing out.

The two roommates were staying at a one-bedroom apartment at 1441 E. Second Street in Tulsa. It was a one-story, cinder block apartment complex with only five apartments.

Pugh and McDonald needed Self to go away, but he had already testified at one grand jury proceeding in the Judge Nelson bombing case that didn't result in any indictments, and he could testify at another, this time swaying the grand just to indict the two men.

Pugh was somehow able to make a copy of Self's apartment key, and wearing trench coats and black ski masks, Pugh and McDonald quietly entered the apartment.

Pugh walked up to Self's bed. Self was passed out drunk, and there was an empty bottle of vodka on the floor. A copy of the book "The Godfather" was opened and upside down on the bed next to Self, saving the place where he had stopped reading.

McDonald looked over Pugh's shoulder and then leisurely walked over to Bourland, who was asleep on the floor. Bourland was a 49-year old, six-time convicted felon who had just gotten out of McAlester's Big Mac prison, and he was fast asleep. He was, more than likely, passed out drunk.

At the bed, Pugh looked at Self and slid off his mask, exposing his face. His hair was messy and filled with static until he took both hands and slicked his hair back into place. He wanted his face to be the last thing Self saw before he died. Pugh wanted Self to know he killed him and to ponder on it for the rest of eternity.

They would probably end up in the same place and be able to discuss it, eventually.

Pugh put his boot on the foot of the bed and gave it a nudge. It moved slightly, but not enough to wake Self. He did it again and got no response.

"Big 'Un!"

"Hey, Big 'Un," Pugh said, slightly louder the second time.

"Hey, Big 'Un!" he shouted.

Self suddenly woke and sat up about halfway. He squinted as he saw Pugh's face. His eyes didn't even have time to focus on the .357 Magnum that was pointed at his cheek.

And that's where the first bullet went, BOOM!

Self's head shot back, and his body slumped back onto the bed in the same position he was in while he was sleeping.

BOOM! BOOM! Pugh shot Self in the face two more times. He made sure Self was dead and an open casket funeral was now out of the question.

His killer then placed a pillow over his face after the shooting.

During the shots, McDonald stared at Bourland without taking his eyes off of him. McDonald knew why they were there, and the gunshots didn't faze him. They didn't faze Bourland either. The roommate didn't flinch after the first shot and his body never moved. The second and third shots didn't wake him either.

McDonald was convinced Bourland slept through the whole thing.

Pugh had several reasons to want Self dead. The two were accused of arson in Little Rock, Arkansas after burning down a nightclub. Both were charged with the crime, but it was lying dormant and no official court date was being pursued. However, the new district attorney of Pulaski County got a hold of some cold cases and, the arson bombing looked ripe to him.

Self had already agreed to testify against Pugh earlier on in the investigation.

The Pulaski County D.A. contacted Pugh's attorney in Arkansas who then contacted another of Pugh's attorneys in Tulsa. That attorney was Charlie Pope, the man that ran against Judge Fred S. Nelson in the previous year's primary election.

The two murderers spared Bourland's life. They put their ski masks on, put their guns in their pockets, and casually walked out of the only door to the apartment.

That next morning, on Tuesday, March 31, 1971, Bourland woke up from his alcohol-induced coma and managed to pull himself up off of the floor. He was hungry and wanted to get breakfast and more alcohol. He yelled for Self but got no answer.

The sound of silence in the apartment was deafening. Self wasn't snoring, and he didn't grunt, moan or roll over in his bed when Bourland hollered at him several more times.

Bourland tightened all of his muscles and put his arms behind his head, grunting and exhaling as he stretched to start the day. He walked up to Self's bed and tried to wake him.

"Big 'Un!"

"Big 'Un, wake up."

There was still no response.

"Big 'Un, come on. Wake up."

He then shook Self and removed the pillow from his face, exposing the three bullet holes and a lot of blood. There was blood coming from Self's nose and from each of the bullet holes on his face. The bedsheet around Self's head and shoulders was soaked in blood.

A panicked Bourland locked the door and got out of the apartment just in case the murderers decide to come back. Plus, there was a dead man in the apartment Bourland was living in and he had no idea how he died. The last time he saw Self, he was alive and lying on the bed, reading "The Godfather." As far as Bourland knew, he was the last person to see Self alive.

He was so upset, he forgot to grab a key to the apartment door, locking himself out.

Terrified and shaken, Bourland called the Tulsa Police Department and met officer R.T. Williams and another officer at a Tulsa café at around 7 a.m., Tuesday, March 31, 1971, and Bourland told the officers what he saw. All three went back to the apartment, and the officers were able to open a window and crawl inside.

The scene was just as Bourland described.

An investigator found two .38 caliber slugs on the ground, and one was still lodged in Self's head. The investigator said it is possible to fire .38 caliber bullets from a .357 Magnum.

The Tulsa Tribune headline on March 31, 1971 stated, "Second Mystery Witness in Nelson Bombing Slain."

It didn't take long for the local news media to find the link between Cleo Epps and Arlis Delbert Self. They both testified against Pugh and McDonald in the Nelson bombing grand jury.

Self was no angel. He was convicted on a federal charge of interstate transportation of a stolen vehicle in 1951, receiving a three-year sentence. In 1956, he got two years for burglary, and 10 more years in 1959 for another burglary conviction. In 1963, he got seven years for shooting with intent to kill but was released in March 1967. He had not been arrested since.

Self's history with the two murderers, Pugh and McDonald, goes back even further with the 1970 Nelson bombing grand jury. Self testified and was the "star witness" in a 1968 Creek County arson case, involving Pugh and Fred McDonald and McDonald's wife. Fred McDonald was the brother of Albert McDonald. It was an arson for insurance money scam, and Pugh and the McDonalds set fire to the McDonald house. Self testified to the fraud.

That same year, Pugh eventually pleaded guilty to a Creek County charge of receiving stolen property, and Self testified in that case, as well.

In an earlier charge, Lester and Mary Jo Pugh were charged in Tulsa County for burglary, and Self testified against them, but the case was dismissed.

Pugh and McDonald were eventually arrested and charged with Self's murder, but they filed for a severance of the trials, and it was granted. Pugh would face a murder trial for the killing Self, first. His trial started on October 12, 1972.

The instructions of the court: "In this case, the defendant stand charged by information filed in this court with the crime of Murder, alleging that the defendant did, on or about the 31st day of March, 1971, in Tulsa County, Oklahoma, and within the jurisdiction of this court, unlawfully, feloniously, willfully, maliciously and intentionally, while acting in concert with another, without authority of law, and with a premeditated design upon the part of said defendant to effect the death of a human being, to wit; one Arlis Delbert Self, shoot and discharge a leaden bullet into the body of him and the said Arlis Delbert Self for a certain loaded pistol which he, the said defendant then and there had and held in his hands and did then and there and thereby inflict upon the body of him the said Arlis Delbert Self, a mortal wound, from which said mortal would the said Arlis Delbert Self did then and there languish and die, contrary to the form of the statutes in such cases made and provided, and against the peace and dignity of the state.

"You are instructed that a severance had been granted in this case, and the only defendant you are to concern yourselves is the defendant Tom Lester Pugh."

On Thursday, October12, 1972, the trial of Thomas Lester Pugh, the death of Arlis Delbert Self, started in the courtroom of Judge Lee West, and S.M.

Fallis and Ronald Shaffer were there for the state, and George Briggs would represent Pugh.

The jury was selected and sworn to try the case. The jurors were: Rayfield Asberry, Mayme B. Gray, Richard Coble, Velma O. Lovett, Hubert Dannatt, Joe Chambers, C.H. McClatchey, Foye Clark, Howard D. Smith, Norman E. Carter, Lawrence Cuinnan and Robert Fisher with alternates Chester E. Wilson and Jesse Anderson.

The jury was then excused from the courtroom and Pugh's change of venue motion was denied.

With the jury back in the courtroom, the state called its first witness, Tulsa Police Officer R. T. Williamson. He testified that on March 31, 1971, he met with Beauford Bourland and officer Don Holcomb at the Savoy Café at Third and Detroit Avenue at 7 a.m. and Bourland told him that Self was dead inside an apartment, located at 1441 E. Second Street, Apartment C. After taking the screen off of a window and opening the window with the blade of a knife, Bourland was assisted into the apartment and opened the door for the two officers.

He told the jury he found Arlis Delbert Self in the northwest corner of the apartment, lying in bed on his back. On the left side of the head there appeared to be three bullet wounds and Self was dead. Williamson said that Sergeant Phillip Roberts and Sergeant Hal Rawlinson arrived at the scene before he left and that Bourland was very intoxicated when he met with him that morning.

He also admitted that Bourland was originally charged with the death of Self, but those charges were dropped.

Sgt. Don Holcomb, of the Tulsa Police Department, was then called to testify the same as Williamson except Holcomb said he checked Self's body for a pulse but couldn't find one. Tulsa Police Department's Lee Nightingale then testified that he went to the crime scene and was responsible for collecting physical evidence, taking photographs and processing the scene for fingerprints.

Nightingale said he found two .38 caliber slugs on the floor beside the bed, and he took photographs of the scene. He was also present when Dr. Robert Fogel took one of the slugs from the head of Self. He also testified that it is possible to fire a .38 bullet from the .357 gun, but the opposite was not possible.

Tulsa Officer Jim Helm was called to the stand and his testimony mirrored that of Nightingale.

Dr. Robert Fogel then took the stand. He is a pathologist employed by the Oklahoma Osteopathic Hospital and a medical examiner in Tulsa, Oklahoma.

He testified that he found five wounds on Self's head – three entry wounds and two exit wounds. Dr. Fogel determined the cause of death was the direct result of the three bullets to the head.

The State then called attorney Charles Pope, who testified that he was acquainted with the defendant, Thomas Lester Pugh, and he had the occasion to meet Albert McDonald and Rubie Charles Jenkins while they accompanied Pugh. He admitted he saw all three in his office and at a cafe.

Convicted felon James Sipes testified that he was a burglar by profession and had been in the business for about five years. He told the jury he had been convicted of misdemeanors and had a pistol hearing in Oklahoma and Arkansas. He also had arrests for drunk, public drunk, speeding tickets, and automobile violations, such as not having a safety inspection sticker.

Sipes testified that he knew Pugh and Pugh informed him of Self's death in early April 1971. He said Pugh told him Self had been shot to death with a .357 magnum. Sometime in November 1970, Sipes was with Pugh and McDonald at the Rio Motel in Tulsa, but they were also accompanied by James Thomas Frasier, another criminal. Sipes said he had a conversation with Pugh about Self. Pugh told him he paid $100 to obtain Self's address and he and McDonald put on ski masks and headed to the apartment, but Self was not there.

Pugh said Self cost him $15,000 and two years of his life and there wasn't any way for Self to pay him back for the two years of his life.

On another date, the three were at the Coachman Inn in Little Rock, Arkansas, and Pugh was giving details about the death of Self.

FALLIS: What did (Pugh) tell you?
SIPES: Well, he told me that he and Al went to his apartment and they were – had ski masks on and black trench coats. He said Al stood watch at the door. Lester

said he went in. He acted all of this out when he was doing it, kind of like he was an actor.

FALLIS: He acted it out?

SIPES: Yes sir.

FALLIS: How do you mean that?

SIPES: Well, he would – he – well, he said he went in; he kicked him on the floor; and he, you know, I guess he kicked him with his left foot.

FALLIS: You mean, he demonstrated this?

SIPES: Yes.

Sipes talked about how Pugh tried to wake Self several times until Self woke up and sat up. He said Pugh said when he went into the room, he already had the gun down to his side and the hammer was cocked and ready. Self woke up, opened his mouth in fright, turned his head to the side, and was shot three times.

FALLIS: Three times?

SIPES: Yes, sir, and on the way out he said Al asked him about -- what about the other one, and (Pugh) says, "Well, he's drunk, and he never did wake up."

FALLIS: Lester was saying this?

SIPES: Yes, sir.

FALLIS: How long were you there in the room with Al McDonald and Lester Pugh and James Thomas Frasier on that evening?

SIPES: I don't know exactly how long it was.

FALLIS: Did you hear any other discussion with reference to the death of Arlis Self while you were there that evening?

SIPES: Yes, sir, Pugh stated that he had a death certificate there, and Frasier read it.

FALLIS: Did you see this, yourself?

SIPES: I didn't read it. I saw a piece of paper. I didn't –

FALLIS: You don't know what the paper was?

SIPES: No sir, I didn't read it.

Sipes then testified to several other occasions where Pugh would either talk about Self's death or admit to killing Self. He also identified the green apartment building where Self was killed. He said Pugh pointed it out to him while they were riding around in Pugh's car.

Now it was Rubie Charles Jenkins turn, and he did not disappoint. Jenkins had a string of charges and convictions against him, and he said he knew Pugh and he often called Pugh long-distance on many occasions.

Jenkins said Pugh told him that someone "had blowed Arlis Self's head off the night before." Pugh said Self was shot three times.

Jenkins then returned to Tulsa, Oklahoma and began spending time with Pugh and McDonald. Pugh told Jenkins he got a key to Self's apartment.

JENKINS: Pugh said that after that day, after he got the key made, later on that evening he and Albert McDonald went back by his apartment. And there still wasn't nobody at home. They unlocked the door and went in the apartment. They left. Later on, that night, they went back by there. Arlis Self's pick up was parked in front of the apartment, and they put on raincoats and ski masks.

FALLIS: Did (Pugh) say what kind of masks?

JENKINS: Ski masks.

FALLIS: All right. And what else did he say.

JENKINS: They went into the apartment. Said there was one man laying asleep or passed out drunk on the floor. Arlis Self was asleep on a bed. Albert McDonald stood over the drunk (man) passed out on the floor. Lester walked in at the end of the bed where Arlis Self was laying.

FALLIS: Did he say what he did then?

JENKINS: Yes, sir. He said he pulled his mask up off his face so that Arlis would be able to recognize him and took his leg there at the foot of the bed, nudged the bed and Arlis's feet, and called him Big 'Un.

FALLIS: Big 'Un?

JENKINS: Yes, sir.

FALLIS: Had you ever heard that before?

JENKINS: Yes, sir. I had heard other people refer to Arlis Self as that.

FALLIS: I see. All right. And what did he say then?

JENKINS: He said Arlis Self woke up, he kind of raise his head up and seen who he was, and Lester said he shot him. The first shot through the left cheek or temple.

He said he went ahead and shot him through the head two more times.

Jenkins then testified that Pugh and McDonald decided to spare the life of the roommate Beauford Bourland, and that Pugh told him he had a .357 magnum.

The convicted criminal also confirmed prior testimony that he went with Pugh and McDonald to the office of attorney Charles Pope in regard to the Arkansas arson case.

JENKINS: On the road there, Lester had told me that Charlie Pope was getting in contact with somebody in Arkansas to get a case dismissed against him that Arlis Self had been a witness against him on. And since Arlis was dead that they were making arrangements to get the case dismissed.

FALLS: I see. And that was the purpose for the trip there?

JENKINS: Yes, sir.

Jenkins did the most damage to the defense by testifying that after Self's murder he went with Pugh and McDonald to see attorney Charles Pope, who was told to get the Arkansas arson case dropped because, now, there were no witnesses.

On cross examination, Briggs asked Jenkins, just like he did the other criminal witnesses for the state, if they had been promised anything for his testimony. Jenkins, like the others, said "No."

The last witness for the state was James Guy Tucker, the prosecuting attorney for the Sixth Judicial District of Arkansas. Tucker was getting ready to prosecute Pugh for an arson in Pulaski County, and Self agreed to testify for the state.

FALLIS: Now, Mr. Tucker, are you familiar with the case that was pending at the time you took office, for the charge of arson against a defendant by the name of Arlis Delbert Self, Tom Lester Pugh, and any other party?

TUCKER: Yes, sir, I am. I'm quite familiar with that case. It's case No. 71677, which –

FALLIS: Now, Mr. Tucker, with reference to the defendant Tom Lester Pugh, do you know who the counsel was that you contacted.

TUCKER: It was Mr. Howell.

FALLIS: Did you say anything to Mr. Howell?

TUCKER: I advised him that I wanted to bring this case to trial as speedily as possible.

FALLIS: Mr. Tucker, do you recall or is it possible for you to tell this court and jury when that particular conversation took place?

TUCKER: Yes, sir, based on the time that I was reviewing these files, it had to have been at the earliest, the latter part of February, the last few days of February, not later than March 20th. I would guess approximately somewhere between March 5th and 10th, somewhere in that neighborhood.

FALLIS: Mr. Tucker, the defendant, Arlis Delbert Self, did he have any particular significance in the case other than the defendant?

BRIGGS: Object to that as incompetent, irrelevant and immaterial; and a conclusion on the part of this witness, improper.

THE COURT: Overruled.

TUCKER: Yes, sir, without the testimony of Arlis Delbert Self, I had no case against any of the other defendants, either those already named or those that I sought to charge in addition. He was my state's witness, and without his testimony, I would have to dismiss the charges against those defendants.

FALLIS: Now –

BRIGGS: We move to strike all of that, if your Honor please, at this time, because they are improper and not within any issue in this case, and prejudicial.

THE COURT: Overruled.

BRIGGS: And we would now move at this time for a mistrial by reason of the misconduct of the State of Oklahoma.

THE COURT: Overruled. Allow the defendant an exception.

FALLIS: Thank you, your Honor. Tucker, what is the status of that case at this time?

BRIGGS: Object to that as incompetent, irrelevant and immaterial.

THE COURT: Overruled.

TUCKER: That case is no longer pending in my district. I had to – the State of Arkansas moved to –

BRIGGS: We object to any further statement as not responsive to this question having already been asked and answered.

THE COURT: Sustained.

BRIGGS: Your Honor, and we ask the court to advise this witness who states that he is a prosecuting attorney, with references to our procedure in this state, with responsiveness to questions.

THE COURT: All right, the court will admonish the witness to respond only to the questions that are asked.

FALLIS: Mr. Tucker, you say the case is no longer pending?

TUCKER: I've nolle prosequi'd the case, declined to prosecute it on June 7, 1971.

FALLIS: And can you tell the court and jury what basis you declined or dismissed the case?

TUCKER: We object to that, your Honor, because it's incompetent, irrelevant, and immaterial, the reasons for this witness why he would nolle prosequi or whatever he says a case.

THE COURT: Overruled.

FALLIS: You may answer.

TUCKER: I had received evidence of the death of Arlis Delbert Self, therefore knew that I no longer had the evidence to present my case in court.

FALLIS: Do you know from whom or what source you received the evidence?

TUCKER: It was presented to my office by Mr. Howell, the defense counsel.

FALLIS: And do you recall what the evidence consisted of, sir?

TUCKER: Yes, sir. It consisted of a certificate of death issued by the State of Oklahoma, which I have in possession.

FALLIS: May I see that, please? (Tucker hands Fallis the piece of paper) Mr. Tucker, I hand you, sir, what has been marked for purposes of identification state's exhibit No. 50. Do you recognize that, sir?

TUCKER: Yes, sir. This is the certificate of death which was provided to my office by Mr. Howell, and which has been maintained in the files of my office until I provided it to you.

FALLIS: Thank you, sir.

Fallis then offered into the record, state's exhibit No. 50, the death certificate of Arlis Delbert Self. Briggs objected on the grounds that the death certificate had no probative value to the case. The objection was overruled, and the death certificate was admitted into evidence.

The defense called, James C. Langley. Now the assistant district attorney for Tulsa County, Langley was the chief public defender at the time of the Self murder. He also represented state's witness James Sipes at one point.

BRIGGS: All right. Now, will you tell us, please, Mr. Langley, if you had any conversations with the district attorney or assistant district attorney with reference to an arrangement as to what Mr. Sipes was going to receive and what sentence he would get with regard to this matter?

LANGLEY: No. There was no agreement.

BRIGGS: I'm sorry?

LANGLEY: No, sir. There was no – no conversation of that effect.

BRIGGS: No conversation, you say, with any of the assistant district attorneys, between you and them, with regard to his – some arrangement made for his later on?

LANGLEY: No. Not as to the disposition of this case.

BRIGGS: All right. Can you tell us, please, if you discussed with the district attorney or any assistant in the district attorney's office, his testimony in any case?

LANGLEY: No, there was no conversation as to what he would say.

BRIGGS: Well, I'm not asking you about the conversations as to what he was to say. I'm asking you with reference to whether or not he would be giving testimony for the state in any other case.

LANGLEY: Well, I knew he would be a witness in this case, but that was all I knew.

BRIGGS: Did you discuss with any of the members of the district attorney's staff at that time that he would be giving testimony in this case?

LANGLEY: No, simply that he might be a witness.

Briggs kept asking the same two questions in many different ways, trying to get Langley to concede that he spoke to Sipes or someone in the DA's office about a deal or about Sipes' testimony. Langley answered the same every time, denying both questions.

The defense also called district attorney S.M. "Buddy" Fallis to the stand and he testified that he was aware of burglary charges against Sipes, and he said that the only interaction he had with any Arkansas authorities was when he picked up Jim Guy Tucker at the airport in connection with this case. He also said he did not make any deals with Sipes for his testimony.

The state called Beauford Bourland, Self's roommate to the stand, and he said he meet Self in the state penitentiary. In March of 1971, Self came to Tulsa from Ardmore and got a motel room. Self saw Bourland walking down the road and he picked him up in his old pickup truck.

On March 29, 1971, the two men got some beer, bread, lunch meat, and chips, and headed out to Keystone Lake in Mannford, Oklahoma, just about 10 miles from Sand Springs down Highway 51. They stayed for an hour and left for the motel, picking up more beer on the way.

They went back to Self's motel room and continued to drink beer. At around 4 p.m., the two met Self's ex-girlfriend Gretchel Davis, a Tulsa County court reporter, at her house and drank more beer. The three ate dinner at Davis' house and then returned to Self's apartment where they consumed even more beer.

The next morning, after cashing a check, Self and Bourland went to the liquor store at around 10 a.m. and bought a fifth of orange vodka. They started drinking immediately and went to Wagoner, Oklahoma where they bought two more pints of vodka.

They went to the lake again and drank all the vodka. That afternoon, Bourland bought more vodka and then two hit several "beer joints" to drink more beer. They went back to the apartment and cracked open the new bottle of vodka before Bourland laid down on the floor and fell asleep.

Bourland testified that during the night he was awakened. He heard the voices of two men, and one was Thomas Lester Pugh. He testified that he heard two shots and the two men then left the apartment. Bourland fell back asleep.

He woke up the next morning and found Self dead on his bed. Bourland ran out of the apartment, still wearing the clothes from the day before, and he located a bootlegger and fortified himself with wine.

He then called the police.

Bourland admitted that drinking had been a continual problem for him and that he was a very heavy drinker.

FALLIS: Starting with Monday the 29th, give us a brief account of the activities of yourself and Arlis Self.

BOURLAND: Me and Arlie ate supper at the county court reporter Gretchel Davis' house. We went back to his house and slept. Tuesday morning at 8:30 or 9 a.m. I went to Trinity Industries to see about a job, but Sam Nelson couldn't see me. I went back to A.D.'s and then we went to Wagoner until later Tuesday evening. We went to Wagoner and Coweta and returned late Tuesday evening. I got another quarter of vodka and we drank it. He laid down on the bed and I laid down on the floor. I woke up (Wednesday) morning and got up. I call A.D. "Big 'Un." I shook him and told him to wake up. I shook him and got no response. I shook him again and told him to get up. I saw he was dead. I went out of the house and locked the door, then went down to the Savoy and called the police. They came and got me and took me back to the house. They opened a window and I crawled in the window and opened the door.

FALLIS: When you went to call the police, was the door locked?

BOURLAND: No, but I locked it when I left.

FALLIS: When you woke up and found A.D. bleeding from the nose and apparently dead as you aforestated, to your knowledge, was the room arranged any different at that time than what it was when you went to bed?

BOURLAND: There was some little pieces of wood or something, I don't know what it was, that was there that wasn't there before.

FALLIS: Bourland, do you have any idea who might have done this?

BOUTLAND: Yes, I think Lester Pugh killed him.

FALLIS: Why do you think this?

BOURLAND: Because he snitched on Lester Pugh four or five years ago. I know it had to be Albert McDonald or Lester Pugh.

The defense also called Lorraine Alcorn, a friend of the Pughs, and she told the jury that her and her husband had visited the Pughs at their Glenpool home on the evening of the murder and stayed from 6:30 to 11:30 p.m. Mary Jo Pugh also testified that her husband was with her the night of the Self murder and the following day.

On Thursday, October19, 1972, at 5:25 p.m. the jury retired to the jury room to decide Pugh's fate. The jury deliberated until 9:30 p.m. and informed the bailiff they had reached a verdict.

The jury foreman Howard Smith stood and handed the bailiff the piece of paper with the verdict written on it. The bailiff handed the paper to Judge West, who looked at it and handed it back to the bailiff, immediately.

Smith was handed the paper. He looked at the judge and looked down, reading what everyone was waiting to hear.

"We, the jury impaneled and sworn in the above entitled cause, do upon our oaths find the defendant guilty as charged in the information herein and fix his punishment at life imprisonment in the state penitentiary."

A Tulsa jury convicted Pugh in the murder of Arlis Delbert Self, and he would spend the rest of his life in prison.

Briggs immediately filed for a new trial with a change of venue.

An Associated Press story read:

Jury Convicts Rancher In Murder Of Witness

TULSA (AP) – A Tulsa County rancher was found guilty Thursday night of murdering Arlis Delbert Self, a 41-year old Tulsa laborer who was a key witness against rancher in a Little Rock, Ark. nightclub arson case.

Tom Lester Pugh of Glenpool sat passively as the verdict of a three-woman, nine-man jury was read after the panel deliberated four-and-one-half hours. The jury recommended life imprisonment.

Pugh now awaits trial for the death of Cleo Epps, former bootlegger and another grand jury witness like Self, and in the bombing, which seriously injured a Tulsa judge.

This was the second murder trial for Pugh. He was acquitted last spring in neighboring Osage County of shooting to death another grand jury witness, Tommy Martin Edwards, of Tulsa.

The state's case depended largely on testimony from a former Pugh friend, Rubie Charles Jenkins, an ex-convict facing a murder trial in California.

Jenkins and an admitted burglar, James Milton Sipes of Arkansas, testified in the four days of testimony here that Pugh and McDonald admitted killing Self.

McDonald is a co-defendant in the Self, Epps and bombing cases, but will stand trial separately.

Pugh wanted Self dead, Jenkins said, because Self was the only witness against him in a North Little Rock, Ark. nightclub arson case in 1968. The charge was dropped after Self's death.

Before the trial, rumors were flying that Pugh would never be tried for the Arkansas arson case because he paid off several Arkansas political figures to "keep him out of Arkansas." One of Pugh's attorneys was a former state senator from Arkansas.

Pugh appealed his decision in case No. F-73-29, but the Oklahoma Court of Criminal Appeals affirmed his conviction and sentence. Pugh was now going to spend the rest of his life in prison.

Cleo Epps

Albert McDonald and Thomas Lester Pugh were charged with the murder of Cleo Epps on November 24, 1971.

After numerous preliminary hearings and motions, the trial didn't actually start until May of 1974. During those hearings, most of the same witnesses testified that eventually testified in the actual trial. Some gave the same testimony, and some didn't. Some of the witnesses told the police one thing, and then later, while incarcerated, remembered a different version. The thing about the witness testimony from a felon facing many years in the penitentiary, they either forget or remember things that may or may not help the prosecution, or the defense, for that matter.

During the preliminary hearings, which mainly took place in 1972 under the watchful eye of Judge Jess Miracle, both sides covered a lot of things, including whether or not Tom Gilbert offered a reward to find Epps's body. The Nelson bombing preliminary hearings were going on at the same time with basically the same witnesses.

The two cases were linked. There is no doubt about that.

Tom Gilbert said in court that he did not offer $10,000 or $25,000 for the whereabouts of his sister, Cleo Epps, but admitted that he said to Everett Collins, an attorney and politician, and Wayne Padgett, a former bail bondsman, that he said he would pay $25,000 if his sister were found alive.

When Jack Sellers, McDonald's attorney, asked Tom Gilbert for his son's name and address so they could serve a subpoena, he said "What are you trying to do, send someone out to get him, too?"

Miracle did not force Tom Gilbert to provide his son's information, and he prohibited Sellers from asking questions about Epps' estate.

Billie Popovich, a friend of Epps' said Epps was at her house when the phone rang and McDonald told her meet him and Pugh at the shopping center parking lot, and John and Loda Bough testified that Epps was at their house eating dinner when McDonald showed up and lured the bootlegger to the parking lot.

Rubie Charles Jenkins testified that he was told McDonald called Epps and told her to meet him at the shopping center.

Georgia Whipple Jenkins testified that her husband said Pugh told him of the Nelson Bombings the week the grand jury ended its probe in early October 1970.

"Lester said that Al had come to him with an offer that they bomb Judge Nelson so Pope would become judge and do favors for them," she said.

She said that no money exchanged hands for his part in the bombing. It was just a favor for McDonald. She also admitted she would apply for the reward money offered by the Oklahoma Bar Association and the Tulsa World.

At one of the Nelson preliminary hearings, Judge Nelson testified to the bombing and what happened that day, and he admitted while being questioned by Sellers that he had received threats while being a judge and while working in the U.S. District Attorney's Office.

Nelson also admitted the district judge race wasn't hotly contested and the candidates didn't throw mud or threats around. He even said he didn't really run a campaign other than supporters, including Sellers. Nelson said he didn't hear anything the night before the bombing when Pugh and McDonald were attaching the bomb to the car's ignition.

The Nelson house was near 41st Street which is a very busy street in Tulsa.

"I hear a lot of strange noises, motorcycles, cars backfiring all day and night," Nelson said.

*****

There were actually four witnesses against Pugh and McDonald, three in the grand jury proceeding, and those three were dead by the hands of the two men. Cleo Epps, Tommy Martin Edwards and Arlis Delbert Self wouldn't live long after their testimony against Pugh and McDonald.

The fourth was Pete English. He died before Edwards' death in a fire that erupted in a tavern in Stillwell, Oklahoma. Some say English was murdered, and others say he died trying to torch the bar. Others say it was just an accidental fire.

English was supposed to have knowledge of some of Pugh and McDonald's criminal activity.

McDonald was convicted of killing Epps, but the murder charge against Pugh was eventually dropped. Pugh was convicted of killing Self, but McDonald was acquitted. Tulsa Country District Attorney S.M. Buddy Fallis agreed to dismiss the charges against Pugh in the Epps murder case and the Nelson car bombing due to the lengthy prison sentences he had waiting for him in four other states for various crimes, including robbery.

Pugh was charged and convicted in the murder of Self, an ex-convict who had a lot of dirt on Pugh and McDonald.

Self's killing sent Pugh to prison, but it all started to unravel after the attempt on Judge Nelson's life.

CHAPTER ELEVEN
The Dixie Mafia

If the walls of the Avalon Supper Club could talk, they wouldn't say a word.

Judges, criminals, lawmen, murderers, business tycoons, arsonists, lawyers, famous actors and musicians, and government officials all rubbed elbows at the Avalon Supper Club, also known as the Avalon Steakhouse.

Open nearly 24 hours a day to accommodate its patrons, the small, cement-block structure was a smoky restaurant and bar where murders were planned, and lawyers made deals for their clients. The building wasn't on the beaten path. It was appropriately nestled in a wooded area between a junkyard and an industrial plant less than a quarter mile from New Sapulpa road, or Route 66, connecting Sapulpa to Tulsa.

The parking lot, made of both dirt and gravel, witnessed as much as the inside walls of the steak house, but it isn't talking either. The Avalon knows what happens to rats.

There was also a white house near the property of the Avalon and Epps' best friend Billie Popovich lived in that house. The house had a chain-link fence around it with barbed wire at the top. It wasn't a fence for decoration. It was to keep people out.

It's rumored that Popovich was a madam that ran a brothel.

The Avalon Steak House originally started in downtown Tulsa as the Cheyenne Club in 1963, but four years later when Tulsa County decided bars had to stop serving alcohol at 2 a.m., the Cheyenne Club moved to Creek County, just across the Tulsa County line near West Tulsa and changed its name to the Avalon.

At the time, Creek County liquor laws weren't as stringent, and even if they were, the county was given the nickname "Crook County" for a reason.

Back then, doors were always locked at the Avalon Steakhouse, but that didn't mean it wasn't open. It meant that, after knocking and standing to where the armed bouncer could see you out of a small peephole, you could get access to the place if he deemed you worthy. The door was then re-locked.

Located at 6304 S. 57th W. Ave, the place was right between the town of Sapulpa and West Tulsa in Creek County, making it an easy pit stop for residents of both areas. The restaurant didn't attract a lot of walk-in customers. The place was so hidden that no one ever just stumbled up on it. Customers had to know it was there which means they knew about its reputation.

The steakhouse was located just down the street from the Oaks Country Club, a ritzy, high-end golf course that started in 1936, and the two businesses couldn't have been more different but often patronized the same cast of characters.

To say the patrons at the Avalon were a bit rough would be a bit of an understatement, and it wasn't uncommon for the Dixie Mafia to conduct business there. Some people have even said it was the unofficial headquarters of the Dixie Mafia for the area.

Carrying a gun or knife was almost a prerequisite, and waitresses couldn't be timid. Some even quit before the end of the shift on their first day. They had to be able to carry themselves and handle the occasional smack on the butt. They also had to help break up fights, and there were always fights.

Also known as "The Gun and Knife Club" to law enforcement, Creek County Deputies often let the patrons sort out their own issues.

Tabbed a place with a "rough and tumble" atmosphere, the Avalon also doubled as a honky tonk with live music, and it had a laundry list of colorful characters with badass attitudes. It also had the best steaks around.

Regular patron Dale Carr would sometimes shoot his guns in the steak house when the mood hit him. He wouldn't shoot at anyone. He just liked to shoot his guns.

It wasn't uncommon for Willie Nelson, David Allan Coe, and Waylon Jennings to stop by for an impromptu jam session at around 2 a.m. after playing gigs at the Cain's Ballroom in downtown Tulsa. There are also a few stories floating around about Tulsa native and Academy Award Nominee Gary Busey.

Oklahoma did not allow "liquor-by-the-drink" and patrons had to bring their own bottle to restaurants or bars, or they could purchase a bottle from the bar. Most bars would write the patrons name on the bottle in black marker and serve them from the bottle during each visit.

However, the Avalon had "liquor-by-wink." They just sold shots of whatever to whoever. Laws weren't actually a thing at the Avalon Steakhouse and it often felt like international waters where no laws existed, and no one was there to enforce them.

The steaks weren't the only things to get bloody at the Avalon. It wasn't rare for a waitress to see a man get stabbed as she was bringing out his food.

In 1984, liquor by the drink was voted in by Oklahomans, and the need for "clubs" faded quickly. The Avalon started to fade, as well.

The colorful characters and less than moral behavior started to wane in the late 1980s, and things slowed down at the place.

On September 18, 1984, Oklahoma was back to serving saloon-style again, one drink at a time, and they were the last state to do so. Proponents of liquor by the drink said it would bring more money to state, but church leaders said drunk driving accidents would increase. It didn't pass overwhelmingly. The 77-year old law was reversed by about 51 percent of the vote.

The dance floor was removed in 1994 and live music was a thing of the past at the Avalon.

The bouncer was long gone by the mid-2000s, and the Avalon officially locked its doors one last time on New Year's Eve in 2006. The owners tried a reboot of the Avalon Steakhouse, just a block away from the original, but closed again for good in 2009.

*****

If the Avalon Steakhouse was the unofficial headquarters of the Dixie Mafia, the Western Capri Motel was the unofficial infirmary.

Owned by Cleo Epps, the Western Capri Motel, located at 5320 W. Skelly Dr. in West Tulsa, had over 40 rooms and charged by the day or the week.

And if members of the Dixie Mafia needed a place to lay low, they were welcomed.

Arils Delbert Self needed a place to recuperate after getting shot several times during a robbery in another state. Epps allowed Self to stay at the motel so he could heal, and he had a lot of down time.

Albert McDonald, who was dating Epps at the time, also stayed at the motel often and used the motel's address when needed. Around this time, McDonald and Self became friends, and Self claims that is when he showed McDonald and Pugh how to build a bomb and attach it to a vehicle.

This, along with testifying against McDonald and Pugh numerous other times, got Self killed.

One summer day, Epps' niece Mary Gilbert, Tom Gilbert's daughter, was hanging out with her Aunt Cleo at the Western Capri when a car pulled up. McDonald and Pugh got out and Cleo calmly said, "Mary, get out of here. Go to the back bedroom and hide. Don't come out."

Aunt Cleo did not want the two men to see Mary for her own safety.

The motel had a swimming pool, and Epps would allow the neighborhood children to swim for free during the hot summer months. It was also located just off of

Route 66 with easy access to I-44, I-244 and the Turner Turnpike.

*****

The rise and fall of the Dixie Mafia in the area was short-lived, but the group of outlaws brought a wave of terror, devastation, and destruction wherever they went.

The criminal outfit basically started in the 1960s and its Tulsa-area downfall was the car bombing of Tulsa County District Judge Fred S. Nelson in 1970. More crimes would be committed after the bombing, but after McDonald and Pugh were behind bars, the group wasn't in the news like they use to be, and they stopped being suspects in every crime committed from Louisiana to Arizona.

The name "Dixie Mafia" was created by an eager newspaper journalist, just like Cleo Epps nickname "The bootleg queen," and both names stuck.

After the grand jury proceeding in 1970, the main characters would find themselves behind bars or dead by the hands of other Dixie Mafia members.

The Dixie Mafia was a criminal operation loosely-based, and not as organized, as the actual Chicago or New York mafia operations that rose to power in the late 1910s and early 1920s. The southern syndicate started in the late 1960s, dealing in fraud, illegal gambling, bribery, drug trafficking, burglary, robbery, theft fencing, extortion, arson, murder for hire. They stayed mainly in Louisiana, Arkansas, Georgia, Alabama, Tennessee,

Texas, Oklahoma, Florida, and Mississippi, but occasionally committed crimes in states like California and Arizona.

When the organization started, it did not have a formal chain of command, and the members did not need to be affiliated with a certain country, family, or bloodline like the Italian mafia.

The group became increasingly famous for contract killings, including the killing of current or former members of the Dixie Mafia. Just like most criminal outfits, there is only one rule: "Do not rat to the police."

Members could do horrible and depraved things to sweet old ladies and the organization wouldn't bat an eye, but if they talked to the police, it was over.

When members got arrested, and didn't become police informants, it wasn't uncommon for Dixie Mafia business to be conducted from prison cells, including, and especially, the Louisiana State Penitentiary, which has been home to many, many Dixie Mafia members. Prison drug operations were very popular in the 1970s, and some drug operations included five different state prisons in five different states at the same time.

On the outside, the group had several, what looked like, legitimate businesses. Antique or resale shops would pop up in southern towns, and they were, more than likely, a front for fence operations.

The organization has even made it to the big and small screens over the years. The Dixie Mafia was featured in the FX Channel TV series "Justified" staring actor Timothy Olyphant, and the 1973 movie "Walking Tall" was based on the life of Tennessee Sheriff Buford Pusser, whose wife was allegedly killed by the Dixie Mafia or State Line Gang.

On August 12, 1967, just before dawn, Sheriff Pusser and his wife, Pauline, were driving out to a disturbance call. Kirksey Nix Jr. and three other men checked into the Shamrock Motel the day before, and they were there to kill Sheriff Pusser. While driving to the call on New Hope Road in McNairy County, a blue 1965 Cadillac drove up beside the couple and opened fire, killing Pauline and injuring Pusser. The men apparently did not know Pauline would be with the sheriff. She was collateral damage. Pusser was shot several times, including a shotgun blast in the face, and he needed several surgeries to restore his appearance.

He spent 18 days in the hospital and returned home to an empty house.

Pusser named Dixie Mafia member Kirksey McCord Nix Jr. as the contractor for his wife's death, but no one was ever brought to justice for her murder. Pusser saw and said he could recognize the main triggerman.

An informant, Arlis Delbert Self, said that Albert McDonald was the man sitting in the front passenger seat of the Cadillac. In an FBI report sent to the OSBI, Tennessee agents were asking for the OSBI's help in murder case No. 5-644, the homicide of Pauline Pusser.

The report names McDonald as the shooter and has McDonald's address at the time of the shooting as the Western Capri Motel, which was owned by Cleo Epps.

Tulsa Police Chief Jack Purdie talked to Epps about the murder of Pauline Pusser, and she told Purdie that McDonald was with her the entire month of August 1967, giving the suspected gunman an alibi. She was identified as McDonald's girlfriend in the FBI report.

Purdie also said McDonald was taken into custody on September 9, 1967 as a federal parole violator. Pusser came to Oklahoma looking for answers but was unable to find any. Pusser observed McDonald in the Tulsa County Jail and said McDonald was not the shooter in the front seat of the Cadillac. He was then shown photographs of McDonald's associates and the widowed-sheriff selected a picture of Kirksey Nix Jr. as looking very much like a man in Cadillac during the murder of his wife.

McDonald was off the hook for the murder, and maybe Epps was telling the truth about spending the month of August with him.

In North Carolina, Self was singing at the top of his lungs. He linked Thomas Lester Pugh to Kirksey Nix Jr. and told authorities of several robberies he and Pugh committed together, often using walkie-talkies during the crimes.

Self also told police, Pugh told him about the murder of Dixie Mafia member John Dillon, who was bashed in the head with a hammer. John Dillon was sitting in the front seat of a car driven by Rubie Charles "Bob" Jenkins and the assassin was riding in the backseat.

The murder was very similar to Epps' killing except the murder weapon was different.

Dillon had made the "FBI's Ten Most Wanted List" during the three years he had gone missing. Dillon started out as a petty criminal but worked his way up to eastern Oklahoma's top gang leaders and his reputation was spreading across the country. He became a big-time player in the dope racket and had been convicted on 10 counts of narcotics violations. He was awaiting sentencing when he mysteriously disappeared in 1961.

In the early morning hours of March 2, 1964, police received a call that Dillon's body could be found in an isolated oil field near Chelsea, Oklahoma. A man, who was attempting to disguise his voice as a woman's asked in a high-pitched tone, "Do you want John Dillon?"

The search began and, after the sun rose, the badly decomposed body of John Dillon was found. His fingers had been removed, and an autopsy revealed that Dillon had been killed from blows to the head by a heavy object.

The caller gave detailed instructions as to where they would find the body. In the oil well, or cistern, Dillon's body was weighed down with 100-pounds of oil field equipment, and a large amount of water had to be pumped from the cistern in order to remove the body, strikingly similar to how Epps' body was found.

Pusser was set to play himself in the movie "Walking Tall," but he died in a car wreck on the way back from signing the contract in California. Some said it was an accident. Some said it wasn't.

Kirksey Nix Jr. was once the purported leader of the Dixie Mafia, becoming one of, if not the, most famous member of the organization. Thanks in part to the notoriety of the movie "Walking Tall" and the crimes he was either convicted of or accused of committing.

Born in 1943, Nix was from Eufaula, Oklahoman but had no trouble committing crimes in other states with the help of other Dixie Mafia associates. He is the son of the late Kirkey M. Nix Sr., an Oklahoma Court of Appeals Judge and state senator. It was rumored that the eldest Nix had a taste for strip clubs, night clubs, and illegal gambling halls, and his son wasn't far behind.

What put the younger Nix behind bars for good was the orchestration of the murder of Mississippi State Judge Vincent Sherry and his wife Margaret. On September 14, 1987, Vincent and Margaret Sherry were relaxing in their Biloxi, Mississippi home when they were shot to death. The judge was shot three times in the face, and his wife was shot in the head four times. Both were killed by a .22 caliber pistol.

An indictment in 1991, after his death, claimed Judge Sherry was linked to a scam, involving Nix where inmates would swindle or extort money from gay men, or straight men that dabbled in the gay lifestyle. The judge was allegedly indirectly involved and skimmed $400,000. Judge Sherry, a sitting state circuit judge at the time of his killing, actually had no association with the criminals but his former law partner was associated with them and had given Sherry the money.

The "lonely hearts" extortion scam was allegedly supposed to make enough money for Nix to buy his way out of prison. The inmates would place ads in homosexual magazines looking for a mate to move in and live with. They would send racy or naked photos to the men and plan a life together. Sometimes, it was just a sexual encounter the men were after. After a relationship was established, the inmate would then ask for money. Often times stating they needed money before they could move from where they were currently living out of state. The lies worked, and lonely men started sending truckloads of cash. Some of the "straight men" were extorted after the inmates threatened to "out" them.

Before the Sherry murders, Nix was already in prison after a conviction for the murder of Frank Corso, a New Orleans grocery store executive. Nix was sentenced to life in prison without parole. He served time at Angola State Prison in Louisiana, several Oklahoma prisons, and was eventually transferred to the United States Penitentiary in Terre Haute, Indiana.

In the February 27, 1971 edition of the Tulsa Tribune, journalist Jim Sellars started putting things together about the strong hold organized crime had on the Tulsa area, and that meant the Dixie Mafia.

Suspicion Grows Organized Crime Has Hold on Tulsa

By Jim Sellars

It could be coincidental that witness Cleo Epps, who testified before a Tulsa grand jury probing the bombing attack on Dist. Judge Fred Nelson, was shot in the head a month later.

It could be coincidental that the In Court Lounge across the street from the courthouse was blown apart while a second grand jury was in session probing the Nelson bombing.

Judge Nelson still walks with a limp and Cleo Epps is silenced forever.

It could be coincidental that both grand juries have demanded and received complete anonymity while a long line of witnesses with criminal records is marched before them.

IT IS NO coincidence, however, that the wave of violence has frightened residents of a city that prides itself on its appearance and prospects for progress.

Suspicion is growing that organized crime, like an insidious cancer, has taken hold.

Admittedly, a bomb blast reverberates farther than a gunshot, but an attack on the life of a judge, the killing of a grand jury witness and a devastating bomb blast on a Sunday night within 100 feet of the courthouse beg the question: Is there a connection?

"There may be," said S.M. Fallis Jr., Tulsa County's frustrated district attorney. "But I don't necessarily think so."

IN AN INTERVIEW with the Tribune, Fallis, Tulsa Police Chief Jack Purdie and Tulsa County's Chief Criminal Deputy Frank Thurman admitted that there may be a connection but dismissed the possibility of nationally organized crime, on the order of the Mafia, being in Tulsa.

Observers close to criminal activity in northeast Oklahoma say it's more the work of an area mob than the Mafia organization.

"There is a certain element involved, we know that," Purdie said.

Certainly, he commented, there is no connection between the bombing of the In Court Lounge and the death of Mrs. Fern Bolding, Bristow Kindergarten teacher, who was blown over the roof of her house last month when a bomb ripped her pickup apart.

Don Bolding, husband of the bombing victim, appeared before the grand jury.

CHEROKEE COUNTY authorities, in whose jurisdiction violence has been no phenomenon in the past several years, have appeared before the secret panel. Bombing incidents in Cherokee County reached the stage in 1969 when Dist. Attny. Bill Bliss Jr. was seriously injured at the time. The time-honored method of explosive devices attached by wire to the ignition of a car.

Bombing is effective, and more importantly, it leaves little or no evidence.

Mrs. Bolding's pick up was shattered beyond recognition. The assailant wanted to make sure the job was done right – and it was.

A FEW NIGHTS before her death, a large quantity of dynamite was stolen from a construction site in east Tulsa.

"That's the thing that scares me," Purdie admitted. *"You don't know how many sticks of dynamite are still floating around this town."*

That same worry extends to patrolmen. Recently two patrolmen chased and caught two teen-aged boys who were speeding through the city. The patrolmen jumped out of their car with shotguns. A case of overreaction?

Perhaps, "But my boys are like this," Purdie said, *making his hands tremble.*

FALLIS, WHO is heading the grand jury investigation and is reticent about its direction, said, "I am not trying to minimize the situation. It is bad; don't get me wrong.

"But when you have a bombing it gets big headlines across the front page. How many armed robberies do we have a week and how publicity do they get?"

His point: violence is nothing new in Tulsa.

However, the nature of violence has been altered to include indirect attack on the law itself. The effect, one courthouse source said, is intimidation.

"I don't think there is any doubt but that the bombings could cause problems with future witnesses," Fallis acknowledged

AT THE SAME time, however, he questioned the responsibility of the media in reporting and speculating on activities of the grand jury.

Told that one attorney has said grand juries have outlived their usefulness, Fallis and Purdie took strong exception.

"The grand jury is the only way I have of serving subpoenas," Fallis argued. "You've seen who has come before the grand jury. Would they come in and testify if we called them on the phone and said, 'Hey come one in, we'd like to talk to you about something?'"

Purdie called the grand jury one of the most effective crime fighting tools at law enforcement's disposal.

OBSERVERS, noting the appearance of witnesses from wide-ranging locations, have concluded that officials are after information of any kind that would offer other clues to solution of any and all bombings regardless of the fact that many of the incidents occurred outside the jurisdiction of Tulsa County.

Beyond the grand jury what means are available? The answer: swift, sure retribution with stiff prison sentences and tight parole policies.

As Fallis pointed out, convicted criminals, when appeals fail, always have the hope of quick parole.

Said Purdie: "How can five business people (Pardon and Parole Board members) go down to the penitentiary in two days to parole 30 or 40 people?"

THE LAW, which supposedly protects the innocent, now leans over backwards for the criminal, Thurman said.

"In the past 10 years the only restrictions have been placed on the citizen," he said.

The citizen who is mugged pay for the criminal's defense, finances his appeal and feeds him while he's in prison.

The bitterness and frustration of the three men was evident in the interview, which rambled on and off the record. The things they wanted to say they could not.

They could not say that they know who bombed Nelson, although sources say they know. They could not say who killed Mrs. Bolding, or who shot Cleo Epps or who bombed the In Court Lounge.

IN THEORY, evidence convicts criminals. In practice, as prosecuting attorneys are aware, what served as evidence a decade ago would be thrown out of court today.

The slightest error in the trial of a case can spell reversal and freedom for a convicted man.

The grand jury may find enough answers, but it failed once, and it may fail again.

Once answer, said John Russell Jr., assistant district attorney in Wagoner County, is coordination of efforts by law enforcement officials.

"This is a multiple-county problem," he said. "And we need the structure for coordination of information. There are people who have the necessary information but are afraid to give it to the right people."

RUSSELL, WHO said he would appear before the Tulsa County grand jury, said a new Crime Commission name by Gov. Hall may help if it is provided with enough funds.

Asking for more money at this time may be as fruitless as criminal investigations have been.

Meanwhile, the impression is that it will take more than money. Phrases like "wholesale crime" and "life is cheap" come to mind, along with one that generations have held as gospel: "Crime does not pay."

Their belief shaken, many people now are wondering whether it indeed pays and how much.

Fallis, Thurman, Russell and Purdie weren't ready to put a name to the group of men planting bombs and killing witnesses, but it was just a matter of time before the "Dixie Mafia" name started showing up in newspaper articles.

Some say the Dixie Mafia is still going strong in the south, specializing in human trafficking, arms trafficking, burglary, money laundering, murder, extortion, and prostitution.

CHAPTER TWELVE
Bombs, Bombs, and more Bombs

Not so Blissful

Cherokee County Assistant District Attorney Bill Bliss was known as a "crusading prosecutor" and was dead set on shutting down illegal pool halls and bars. Even the ones that made an attempt to look legitimate were in his crosshairs. Some bars served liquor by the drink and some served illegal whiskey and moonshine.

Other clubs and bars had legitimate services in the front of the building but were nothing more than private gambling halls in the back.

On Saturday, June 14, 1969, the 33-year old Bliss walked out to his truck that was parked in the garage of his red brick ranch-style house. Bliss had been on vacation for about a week and headed out to see his father Judge C.F. Bliss.

A.D.A. Bill Bliss lived in the northwestern section of Tahlequah, and he often visited his father. Bliss' four-year old son, Billy, wanted to go to, but he had to stay home with his mother, Joyce, and a cousin that was visiting.

Billy went with his dad everywhere, and he wanted to go see his grandfather. The boy would normally hop in the truck, put his head on the dashboard and watch the world pass by, looking through the windshield. He would hardly blink. He didn't want to miss anything.

But not this time. Billy had to stay home.

"(The boy) would have been killed for sure," said Highway Patrol Lt. Don Mentser.

However, young Billy didn't walk away unscathed. Sulking a little bit, Billy was standing near the truck so he could watch his father drive away from the house.

Bill Bliss put his keys in the ignition and turned the switch to "on." The bomb blast hurled young Billy into the air and sent metal flying in every direction. The blast destroyed Bliss' truck and part of his home, knocking a hole in the roof of the garage and shattering windows.

Billy was unhurt but dazed, and the truck was smoking and starting to smolder with small fires and hot spots. The hood of the truck was blown into little pieces, and the firewall was completely damaged. The force of the blast was centered around the truck's manifold.

Bliss felt an unimaginable pressure to his face, and he thought, for just a second, his face had been ripped off. Something hard hit him in the mouth, and his chest and jaw felt like they were on fire.

He knew immediately a bomb had just gone off in his truck.

The assistant district attorney had shrapnel blasted into his body, ripping a hole in his side. An artery on his arm was slashed open and bleeding profusely, and the tips of two of his fingers were blown off. Bliss also had several teeth knocked out, and pieces of metal were embedded into his flesh from his chest to his jaw. He had cuts to his face and large gashes were exposed on his legs.

He leaped from the driver's side and staggered away from the truck that could possibly explode, again. He didn't know how many bombs were planted in the vehicle. Bliss grabbed his side that was split wide open and held onto whatever was still there. He thought his insides would fall out if he didn't hold them in place.

Bliss was losing a lot of blood, but he was still alive and was rushed to the Tahlequah City Hospital. Around-the-clock guards were placed outside of Bliss' hospital room in case any other assassination attempts were planned.

Apparently, Tahlequah was no stranger to bombings over the past three or four years, but those were directed at empty buildings for insurance money or land disputes. This bomb was put in Bliss' truck by a would-be killer.

In December of 1967, three private clubs in the area of Tahlequah were blown to bits by dynamite within five minutes of each other. The bombings were never solved, but Bliss was attempting to crack down on open saloon (liquor by the wink) and gambling violations in the private clubs and pool halls.

Club owner Garland Rex Brinlee Jr. opened a club and bar in Tahlequah in 1968 to the protest of Bliss who was trying to get a handle on the clubs. That's when the adversarial relationship began.

After the blast, Brinlee spoke with newspaper reporters and denied having any involvement with the bombing. He spoke of his respect for Bliss but admitted they were at odds and said they had butted heads just six weeks prior.

Apparently, Brinlee put go-go dancers in one of his clubs, and Bliss was not pleased. He even admitted that he called Bliss' office that week and was told Bliss was on vacation.

"As many people as he has stepped on in the last couple of years, it didn't surprise me a bit hat somebody tried to get him. But my club is the only one operating now. Why should I go after him?"

Brinlee was right, his club was the only one operating in the Tahlequah area. The others were all blown up by dynamite.

As Bliss laid in his hospital bed at the Tahlequah City Hospital, he thought about quitting law, altogether, but if he did, law and order would be shot to hell. His wife, Joyce, encouraged Bliss to stay on as an assistant district attorney, and he had her full support.

Bliss looked down at his right hand that was wrapped in so much white gauze it looked like a large white club at the end of his wrist. When he talked, his tongue would occasionally rub the gums where two of his teeth used to be, but all he could talk about were his children, Billy, 4, and Angela, 9.

His two kids were by the truck when the bomb ripped through him, and they could have been killed. That's when Bliss got upset. It wasn't about him or the truck. He could be planning a funeral for one or both of his children.

And for what?

The stocky prosecutor spoke with rage and anger when talking about the possibility of his kids being hurt. Tears swelled up in his eyes.

"If someone's got a grudge against me, they've had plenty of time and opportunities to catch me out away from my family."

By now the tears were streaming down his cheeks.

"It's sorry when they jeopardize your family, your loved ones and your home with something like this. I don't think I knew anyone that sorry, but I guess I do. My children don't even want to go home."

Now sitting up on the bed, and speaking through clenched teeth, Bliss said, "I want the courts to take my revenge – that's where my remedy lies."

"I'm at the Library!"

Garland Rex Brinlee Jr. was a plumber and night club operator in Tahlequah, Oklahoma in the early 1970s. He often played to role of bouncer at his own clubs and bragged about "cracking skulls" when a patron got violent or out of hand.

He was the chief suspect in a stolen truck case, where he allegedly stole a pick-up truck from a used car lot. Brinlee was a pudgy man with straight reddish-blond hair that ended right above his eyebrows. He parted his hair on the right side, exposing a large forehead with a receding hairline. He had a round face with a double chin and his nose was rounded. Brinlee was quite short at 5-foot-5, and his belly often tested the limits of his belt.

Brinlee was no stranger to law enforcement and he was suspected of being involved in an actual stolen car ring in the Tulsa area.

Tahlequah is no stranger to crazy times. It's home to Northeastern State University and is considered a "college town" in every sense of the phrase. With the Illinois River nearby, college students often grab several cases of beer and float the river just as soon as it's warm enough in the spring. The Illinois River is a 145-miles long tributary of the Arkansas River, and Tahlequah is a tourist destination with several resorts, complete with cabins, hiking, camping, and floating expeditions.

Tahlequah, located in Cherokee County, is home to the Cherokee Nation and is nestled in the Ozark Mountains.

Brinlee owned the night club "The Library Club" and it was perfect for college students in the 1970s that were brave enough to enter, but it was a private drinking club for the thirsty and notorious. Since then, versions of The Library Club have opened in Tahlequah, including the "Neon Library" in the early 1990s.

Whatever version, the name was perfect for Tahlequah. If a student's mother called them and said, "What are you doing tonight, son?"

"Oh, I'll be at the Library until late tonight," he would reply.

Fraternities and sororities do not have Greek houses on campus, which means there are a lot of "rent house" parties that go on, or the Greeks meet up at bars to drink and have a good time.

Tahlequah has never had a shortage of bars. If it's a college town, there will be bars, legal or otherwise. Ned's is probably the most famous bar in Tahlequah, and, throughout the years, there's been, Buzzard's Roost, Snoopy's, Buster's, Granny's Attic, The Squeeze Inn, and many, many more.

There's been a rumor floating around since the 1960s that Northeastern State University, which was Northeastern State College until 1974, was once listed on Playboy's list of Best Party Colleges. And even better rumor is that Northeastern State University was No. 1 on Playboy's list of Best Party Colleges, but unfortunately, neither are true.

However, that didn't stop fraternities and sororities from using that rumor to get new members, pledges, neophytes, maggots, whatever they liked to be called.

NSU started in 1851 before statehood as the Cherokee National Female Seminary, and, in 1909, after statehood, the name was changed to Northeastern State Normal School. In 1921, it changed to Northeastern State Teachers College and then to Northeastern State College.

NSU has always been known as a "teacher's college," and, apparently, teachers know how to party.

One of Hollywood's brightest stars, Bamboo Harvester, who was a legend from 1961 to 1966 is buried in Tahlequah. Bamboo Harvester played Mister Ed in the CBS television series "Mister Ed." Bamboo Harvester was a horse.

The horse died in the 1970s and was allegedly buried under a tree with a horseshoe nailed to the tree as a grave marker. However, in 1990, twenty years after his death, Bamboo Harvester got an official granite tombstone paid for by fans of the show. A different story has the horse dying in California in 1970. He was cremated and his ashes spread in a secret place.

Who knows?

In Tahlequah, Brinlee owned clubs, The Library Club, and the Keg, and he owned an apartment complex for college students.

In January of 1971, Rex Brinlee Jr. stopped at the apartment of one of his tenants, Ralph Lee Hinkle, a local college student that was employed by Brinlee. He needed to leave something with the college student. Brinlee had four blocks of C-4 explosives and several blasting caps, putting them in a closet in Hinkle's apartment.

On Monday, February 1, 1971, Brinlee then asked Hinkle to borrow a car so they could practice wiring an explosive to the ignition, and they employed the help of Archie Dale Miller, a Vietnam veteran with explosive experience.

Hinkle borrowed a 1969 Chevrolet pickup and the three men drove to an abandoned house north of Tahlequah. Focusing on the wires of the ignition switch, Brinlee was taught how to place the bomb under the truck, using tape and alligator clips.

The next day, in the early morning hours of Tuesday, February 2, 1971, Hinkle and Brinlee drove to Bristow, Oklahoma, and placed a bomb under the driver's seat of Donald Bolding's truck. Hinkle stood guard with a sawed-off shotgun, and Brinlee crawled under the truck and attached the very large explosive to the ignition switch just like he was taught, using tape and alligator clips.

Donald Bolding was the main witness against Brinlee in the theft of a truck from a used car lot in Tulsa, Oklahoma several months before.

That cold morning, Tuesday, February 2, 1971, Don Bolding was driving to work in his wife's car. The nearly 40-mile round-trip drive from his house in Bristow, Oklahoma to Ellsworth Freight in Stroud, Oklahoma was starting to make a dent in the Bolding's expenses, and his wife Fern Bolding agreed to trade vehicles.

Fern Bolding worked in town, and her car was considered an economy car and was better on gas mileage. She would drive Don's truck to work and her husband would drive her car to Stroud.

Fern Bolding, a 28-year old elementary school teacher at Bristow, taught around 45 kindergarten students at Washington Elementary School. She was a beautiful woman with short brown hair and a pretty smile that could light up a room. She had been teaching at Washington for about five years and was well-respected. She loved the kids and the kids loved her in return.

Classes started at 8:30 a.m. and Fern Bolding took her 5-year old to school every morning. It was a cold February morning, and she went out to warm up the 1971 light green pickup truck before the two headed off to school.

At around 7:45 a.m., Fern Bolding slid onto the seat of the pickup and put the key in the ignition. It was bitterly cold, and she wanted to start the truck and get back inside to her five-year old daughter, Kim.

As she turned the key, an explosion sent the truck in all different directions, but mainly up towards the sky. The huge blast sent the truck and Fern Bolding over her own house and onto the lawn of a neighbor. The truck could only be described as shredded, and the bomb that was placed under the driver's seat and attached to the ignition was intended to kill the driver of the truck.

Fern Bolding was now dead.

Don Bolding hadn't even pulled into the parking lot a work yet and was still driving on the highway when one of his employers waved him down on the road leading to the freight company, telling him to get back to his house, immediately.

Washington Elementary School Principal Codean Holderby was driving to school when he was pulled over by a Bristow Police Officer. The officer told him about the bombing and his teacher's death.

As the officer walked away, Holderby sat in his car in silence. There was nothing to say. He was in shock.

Back at the school, Holderby had Fern Bolding's aide take over the class.

The blast was described as "tremendous" by neighbors, and parts of the truck were scattered over a 100-yard radius and the windows in neighboring houses were blown out.

A neighbor of the Boldings, Clifford Peritt, rushed into the house and picked up Kim, who was terrified after the loud boom. He carried her out of the house, comforting her in an attempt to calm her down. Before running out, Peritt used his feet to stamp out a small fire that started in the kitchen.

On October 17, 1970, Don Bolding, who is the brother of Tahlequah Police Chief Gene Bolding, purchased a vehicle at Swinson Chevrolet, located at 732 S. Cincinnati Avenue in Tulsa. He was scheduled to testify in a preliminary hearing on Friday, February 5, 1971. The bombing occurred three days before the hearing was to take place.

Don Bolding, a 30-year old truck driver, was looking at cars at Swinson Chevrolet when he saw Rex Brinlee Jr. looking at trucks in the parking lot. Brinlee stood out due to his height and he was wearing a brown jacket. Bolding only saw Brinlee for about five minutes, but he noticed Brinlee was looking at a white over yellow pickup truck with an open-road camper on the back. The color was more of a mustard yellow.

That night, Swinson Chevrolet manager, Alfred Harmon, gathered up all of the truck keys and took them to the main office to lock them up. It was a Saturday, and the lot wouldn't be open until Monday morning at around 8 a.m.

On Monday, October 19, 1970, Harmon went to retrieve the truck keys from the office and noticed a set was missing. The missing ignition and door keys were to a three-quarter ton, mustard-yellow over white truck with an open-road camper. Harmon went out to check on the truck and it was missing, too.

During the stolen truck investigation, a Beatrice Coppetti Jones, of Tahlequah was arrested December 1, 1970, while driving the stolen truck from Swinson Chevrolet. She was pulled over for a defective taillight. She was charged with knowingly receiving stolen property, but that charge was dismissed December 17, 1970 by Judge. C. F. Bliss, the father of Tahlequah's Cherokee County Assistant District Attorney Bill Bliss, who narrowly escaped death when his pickup truck was rigged with a bomb that exploded in Tahlequah in 1969. Chief Bolding was the chief investigator in the Bill Bliss bombing.

Judge C. F. Bliss Jr. said that "although there is no question that she had possession, there is a total lack of evidence that she knowingly accepted stolen property."

Beatrice Jones was a free woman, again.

It was also reported the Chief Bolding had been attempting to close any of the Tahlequah night clubs Brinlee was associated with, The Library and The Keg, both were located north of Tahlequah.

Brinlee was arrested after the 1969 Bill Bliss truck bombing but was released the day after, and no charges were filed at that time.

Don Bolding had been driving his truck for nearly three months when he decided to change vehicles with his wife only days before the explosion.

The bomb was intended for Don Bolding.

Bristow, located in Creek County, is about 30 miles southwest of Tulsa, and Bristow Police, the Creek County Sheriff's Office, the OSBI, ATF, and the FBI all helped with the case.

When officers arrived at the Bolding house, they converged on the twisted metal in the driveway and the truck keys were still dangling from the ignition switch. The key was turned to the "on" position.

The Bolding's house, which was painted white, was scorched from the heat of the blast, and several fires started in the Bolding yard, as well as several neighbor's yards.

That afternoon, twisted pieces of metal were sent to the Bristow armory where OSBI agents could attempt to reassemble the sections of truck in order to scientifically investigate the explosion.

Dr. Robert Fogel also performed an autopsy that Tuesday afternoon.

Investigators were already looking into the theft of explosives from a construction company in Muskogee, a neighboring town of Tahlequah, where Brinlee lived.

Hundreds of pounds of explosives that belonged to A&A Construction Co. of Muskogee, of Lynn Lane and 21st Street, were recently stolen along with several boxes of blasting caps, a box of instant electric blast caps, which could be set off by a car's ignition switch.

The explosives included 17 cases, or 850 rounds, of powder primers. The primers, coming 35 sticks to a case, are twice as powerful as dynamite. Pellite Prell, a premixed ammonium nitrate granulated explosive was also taken.

Sue Rush McInnis, Epps' second cousin, said that several months before the Bolding bombing, she had several friends that were hunting in Tahlequah when they came upon a shed out in the woods. They entered the shed and found several cases of dynamite and several boxes of blasting caps. They took two cases and some blasting caps but didn't know what to do with it.

The boys returned to Sapulpa and took it to Cleo Epps, who locked the cases and blasting caps in one of her sheds.

The death of Fern Bolding was the second murder of a Bristow teacher in the span of a year. The bodies of Beulah Bath, 60, and Ray Bath were found in their rural home August 7, 1970. Both had been shot in the chest with a 16-gauge. Beulah Bath was a Bristow Elementary teacher and her husband was a rancher. There was a struggle at the residence and money and possibly credit cards had been taken from a purse and wallet. A spent 16-gauge shotgun shell was found at the scene.

The husband's dead body was found in the master bedroom of the house, and Beaulah Bath's body was found in the dining room. Two shotguns from the ranch were missing.

The two crimes were never linked.

After a preliminary investigation into the Bolding bombing, it was determined that at least 16 sticks of dynamite were used in the blast that killed Fern Bolding. Investigators found lead wires from a blasting cap and alligator clips; the same alligator clips used by Miller when he showed Brinlee how to connect the bomb on an ignition.

Murder charges were filed against Brinlee at around 4:55 p.m. on Friday, June 4, 1971, right as the courthouse was about to close for the day. The suspected murderer was taken into custody around 9 p.m. that night.

On Saturday, June 5, 1971, Brinlee was arraigned and ordered held without bond for the murder of Fern Bolding, however, he was immediately turned over to federal authorities for a fraud case in the state of New Mexico. In that case, Brinlee was accused of falsifying a Federal Aviation Administration application for a pilot's license.

U.S. District Court Judge Howard Bratton, of New Mexico, said Brinlee was to be turned over to U.S. Marshals and returned to New Mexico for the trial that starts Monday, June 7, 1971. After the fraud trial, Brinlee was immediately transferred back to Creek County to face the murder trial.

There is a Creek County Courthouse in Bristow, but the main courthouse for the county is located in Sapulpa, the county seat. Due to the excessive, and warranted, press coverage from the Tulsa TV News stations, as well as the Sapulpa Daily Herald, the Bristow newspaper and the Tulsa World and Tulsa Tribune newspapers, Brinlee filed for a change of venue, and it was granted. The trial was moved to Okmulgee,

Oklahoma, a town located on Hwy 75 about 32 miles from Bristow.

Okmulgee was a more rural community and far enough away from Bristow that an impartial jury could be achieved. Brinlee and his lawyers wanted a second change of venue to be Albuquerque, New Mexico.

On October 27, 1971, a second change of venue motion was filed, but it was denied.

The voir dire of the jury panel in BRINLEE vs. THE STATE OF OKLAHOMA started November 15 and the trail ended Friday, November 19, 1971.

In closing arguments, U.S. Attorney General Paul Ferguson described Brinlee as "cold-blooded" and said, "he deserves to have his body blown to bits."

The defense immediately asked for a mistrial. It was denied.

At around 6:55 p.m., the jury had a verdict. After deliberating for only three hours, the all-male jury found Brinlee guilty in the murder of Fern Bolding, and they recommended life in prison. The state asked for the death penalty, and they were disappointed they didn't get it.

The convicted murderer was obviously dejected when the verdict was read, and he didn't take kindly to the sentence. He looked at his attorney Thomas Dee Frasier and said, "Well, Tiger, I knew the publicity would get us."

But he wasn't finished. Brinlee went down swinging, literally.

As he was being led out of the courtroom, Brinlee punched TV News cameraman Richard Wilson, and he kicked and lunged at Tulsa World Photographer Don Hamilton.

Brinlee was still "cracking skulls."

He started serving his life sentence at the Oklahoma State Penitentiary in McAlester, Oklahoma on November 29, 1971, but he would be free again, twice.

He was also convicted for the stolen truck from Swinson Chevrolet and received a 4 to 12-year sentence.

In August of 1972, Brinlee's wife filed divorce on the grounds of "Incompatibility and extreme cruelty." In the court documents, she asked for custody of their 13-year old son, a 700-plus acre ranch in Mayes County, equipment, tools, trucks, and livestock on the ranch. She also asked for a 38-unit apartment complex in Tahlequah, a steakhouse, bar and nightclub, properties north of Tahlequah, a store in Tulsa, two lots in Tulsa, a lot and cabin on Grand Lake, and a Cessna Skyhawk airplane.

Brinlee escaped from the Oklahoma State Penitentiary during the 1973 prison riot. On Friday, July 27, 1973, five prisoners jumped several guards in the mess hall and a riot ensued. By the time it was over, three people were dead, there were $20 to $30 million in damages, which included the destruction of numerous buildings that burned to the ground. Hostages were taken and eventually released.

Brinlee escaped during his appeal and was on the run when the appeal was heard.

The appellate documents said, "Appellant, Garland Rex Brinlee, Jr., was convicted in the District Court of Okmulgee County, Oklahoma, Case No. CRF-71-115 for the offense of Murder and was sentenced to serve life in the state penitentiary. From that conviction his appeal to this Court has been perfected.

"However, this Court has been advised by the Warden at the Oklahoma State Penitentiary at McAlester, Oklahoma, that on or about the 6th day of August 1973, appellant escaped from confinement in the state penitentiary and now remains at large. This Court has long held that an appeal from a conviction will be dismissed where the accused is a fugitive from justice, or otherwise beyond the jurisdiction of the Court."

Brinlee's appeal was dismissed.

He was captured working as a plumber in Biloxi, Mississippi, a popular city for the Dixie Mafia, and he was returned to McAlester on September 25, 1973.

In 1976, he escaped again through a utility tunnel with six other inmates. He surrendered a few days later in a grocery store.

Garland Rex Brinlee Jr. died December 18, 2009 at Tulsa Saint Francis Hospital at the age of 75. He was transferred to the Tulsa hospital four days before his death. He died of natural causes and is buried at Memorial Park Cemetery in Tulsa, Oklahoma.

"I'm In Court!"

Two grand jury proceedings – one in 1970 and another in 1971 -- with witnesses Cleo Epps, Tommy Martin Edwards and Arlis Delbert Self led to their murders.

After the first grand jury hearing in September of 1970 ended without indictments, Albert McDonald and Thomas Lester Pugh seemed to be in the clear in the Nelson bombing case.

District Attorney S.M. "Buddy" Fallis decided to convene the second grand jury into the Nelson case, and McDonald and Pugh couldn't take any chances. The grand jury started in late February 1971, and Fallis needed to indict the two criminals so they could pay for trying to kill a local judge.

Cleo Epps had been missing since right after the first grand jury proceeding and wouldn't be able to testify, but Edwards and Self needed to do it one more time.

The In Court Lounge was an easy hangout for witnesses that were going to testify or had already testified at the Tulsa County Courthouse. It also became a local hangout for lawyers, judges, and criminals.

The name was especially creative because it could be used as a truthful lie. If a lawyer's wife called him and said, "Where are you?"

He could smile and say, "I'm In Court!" and he wouldn't be lying.

Located at 501 S. Denver Avenue across from the Tulsa County Courthouse, the little shotgun bar, was a popular watering hole for criminals, lawyers, and judges. The In Court Lounge did not discriminate against sinner or saint, and cash was always accepted.

A shotgun house is described a long narrow house, and if anyone was to fire a shotgun into it, the buckshot would travel through the front door and out of the back without doing any damage. A shotgun bar was the same. It was basically a shotgun house that served booze.

It was also located directly across from the courthouse and those practicing or receiving the legal arts did not have to walk far to get a shot of whiskey or a tall glass of beer.

The front of the bar was unassuming. The signage at the top of the building was a long and narrow horizontal sign with black letters that read, "In Court Lounge." The sign was bookended with two square red Coca-Cola advertisements. A two-foot tall white awning sat atop the front door made of glass and was the length of the building. There were also two square windows on each side of the door and neon Coors Light signs in each window buzzed and hummed in front of curtains that shielded the bar patrons from the outside world.

On Sunday, February 21, 1971 a blast ripped through the one-story concrete-block building.

That same day, a snowstorm dumped almost two-feet of snow in parts of Oklahoma. Snow drifts were described as "overwhelming," and roads were icy and dangerous.

The blast was reported from Tulsans that lived more than 10 miles away from the little one-room bar. Support beams in the ceiling were badly damaged and insulation, wires, and part of the drywalled ceiling hung down.

A small fire started from the blast and began growing increasingly as police and fire crews started getting calls about the blast. Luckily, a fire truck was in the area after putting out an unrelated fire,

Tulsa Police and fire responded, and police officers roped off the area. Spectators and news reporters started walking up to the area, but officers wouldn't let anyone close. Investigators were collecting evidence, but the snowstorms were making it harder.

The building itself was not completely knocked down, but a large part of the wall was caved in, and part of the roof collapsed exposing a portion of the top of the tavern. Water and snow leaked into the bar, making an even bigger mess.

Bar operator Larry Miller decided to close the tavern early due to the snowstorm. He locked the front door at around 6 p.m. After Miller closed the bar, an explosive device was placed between the retaining wall and the south wall of the lounge. The building actually had two rooms, one was the bar, the In Court Lounge, and the other a private club, The Tulsa Bridge Club.

Police officials and district attorney Fallis contacted Miller who said he didn't know why the bar was destroyed and couldn't think of any enemies that would want to do harm to the business. Robert Lebus, of Catoosa, Oklahoma, was listed as the owner of the tavern.

An ammonium nitrate sack, a type of material used in explosives, was found at the scene, and Fire Marshal Roy Gann started investigating immediately. Gann was becoming an expert and also investigated the Nelson car Bombing around six months earlier.

The blast knocked out windows at the courthouse across the street, and several 100 windows were shattered at the YMCA, located just south of the bar at the end of the block on Denver. The Tulsa County Library had several large windows broken, and the Fairmont Mayo and Adams Hotels had damage.

It was a common meeting place for attorneys to unwind after court, and, in 1971, liquor by the drink was not legal yet. Several bottles were found away from the building, and the bottles had the names of attorneys written on them in black marker.

The blast that destroyed the bar occurred the same week Cleo Epps' body was found at the bottom of a cistern.

CHAPTER THIRTEEN
The Murder Trial of Cleo Epps

On November 24, 1971, Albert McDonald and Thomas Lester Pugh were both charged in the death of bootlegger Cleo Epps in court case CF-71-2170.

The charge reads: "Be it remembered that S.M. Fallis Jr., the duly qualified and acting district attorney for Tulsa County, Oklahoma, who prosecutes in the name and by the authority of the State of Oklahoma, comes now into the District Court of Tulsa County, State of Oklahoma, and gives the Court to understand and be informed that THOMAS LESTER PUGH and ALBERT MCDONALD on or about the 12th day of November, A.D. 1971, in Tulsa County, Oklahoma and within the jurisdiction of the Court, did unlawfully, feloniously, willfully, maliciously and intentionally while acting in concert each with the other, without authority of law and with a premeditation design upon the part of said defendant to effect the death of a human being, to-wit: on CLEO EPPS, shooting discharge a leaden bullet in the body of the said CLEO EPPS, from a certain loaded pistol which the said defendant then and there had and held in his hand and did then and there inflict upon the body of her the said CLEO EPPS, a mortal wound, from which said mortal wound the said CLEO EPPS did then and there languish and die."

The case would see a bevy of motions on both sides, including the right for McDonald to see his wife while he was in jail, awaiting trial.

On March 29, 1972, Judge Miracle granted a motion for Mary Bishop McDonald, McDonald's wife, to have visitation with McDonald at the Tulsa County Jail for at least 30 minutes during regular visiting hours each Friday.

On April 11, 1972, Thomas Lester Pugh submitted a motion to severe the trial. He wanted to be tried separately for the death of Epps. He was represented by Tulsa attorneys Thomas G. Hanlon and George Briggs.

The motion stated: "The defendant (Pugh) alleges there are acts, declarations and conduct which the State proposes to offer during the course of the trial which could be admissible only against one of the moving defendants and that it would be impossible for the jury to consider said evidence only the declarant or actor, that property seized, if admitted into evidence, would evidence as against one of the defendants and if the other tried with him, it would be highly prejudicial to him and in violation of his constitutional rights afforded by Article II, Section 20 of the Constitution of the State of Oklahoma and the 14th Amendment to the United States Constitution.

"If the defendants were tried jointly with each other, they would be deprived of their right to call said defendant as a witness on his behalf upon the trial of the information as such person may testify only upon their own request, and movant would have no control over their discretion in that respect.

"Should co-defendant, if tried jointly, with the movant elect to testify upon the trial of information, he would have such an interest in the outcome of the case as might influence the jury unfavorably against him in determining the credibility whereas, if movant were tried separately, such defendant, in testifying of the movant, would have a different and less personal interest in the out of the movant's case, and the jury, in determining his credibility, would not be unduly influenced by his personal interests therein; the interest of a defendant on trial in the out of criminal case necessarily being greater than that of a witness who is not himself on trial.

"WHEREFORE, the defendant prays this court grant him a separate trial in the above entitled case.

In July 1972, McDonald's attorney Jack Sellers, of Sapulpa, also filed a motion of severance, stating the same issues.

The severance was granted, and McDonald and Pugh would be tried separately for the murder of Epps. McDonald would be tried first in CRF-73-33, and the jury was told by the judge that McDonald's guilt or innocence was all they needed to concern themselves with.

On July 24, 1972, a witness list for the prosecution was filed in district court, and it included: Dr. Robert Fogel, Georgia Jenkins, James Milton Sipes, Mr. and Mrs. John Bough, Jack McKenzie, Tom Gilbert, Frank Thurman, Tom Lewallen, Frank Vincent, Harvey Sollars, and Chief Jack Purdie.

On January 19, 1973, Sellers filed a motion for a change of venue on McDonald's behalf. The motion was directed at the Honorable Lee R. West, the assigned district judge.

"The accused Albert McDonald hereby makes an application for removal of this cause from this county to another county outside this judicial district for the reason that the minds of the inhabitants of Tulsa County and Pawnee County which comprise this judicial district are so prejudiced against the defendant as a result of the newspaper, television and radio publicity..."

Sellers was right. The Tulsa World and Tulsa Tribune Newspapers printed numerous articles about the Cleo Epps murder from the time her truck was found in the Warehouse Market parking lot right up to the trial, and, eventually, well after. Newspaper, television and radio covered the case, religiously and rightfully so. Everyone wanted to know what happened to the Queen of the Bootleggers.

On February 1, 1973, Judge West ordered the change of venue to the District Court of Bryan County. The Honorable Alan B. McPheron would be the presiding trial judge.

The order read: "Now on this 1st day of February 1973, the defendant, Albert McDonald appears in person and by his attorney, Jack Sellers, and the state appears by S.M. Fallis, the district attorney and by Ronald Shaeffer, the assistant district attorney. Upon application of the defendant, Albert McDonald, for a change of venue, the court, after hearing evidence and for good cause, finds the application should be sustained.

"IT IS THEREFORE ORDERED, ADJUDGED and DECREED that the venue of the above matter be changed to the District Court of Bryan County, Oklahoma; all as per ordered."

The murder case of Cleo Epps was moved from Tulsa to Durant, Oklahoma, a town that is nearly three hours away. Durant is located at the southernmost part of Oklahoma and it borders the state of Texas. The city is just about as far away from Tulsa as one could get and still be in the state of Oklahoma.

The Bryan County Courthouse, in Durant, Oklahoma, is located at 4th Avenue and Evergreen Street. Built in 1917 and designed by architect Jewell Hicks, who was also one of the designers of the state capitol, the beautiful three-story courthouse sits on less than once acre and was listed on the National Register of Historical Places in 1984.

The courthouse is a beautiful white building with four large pillars in front, and there are old lamp posts on each side of the front door.

There is also a large monument in front of the courthouse that celebrates the town's southern heritage.

The white marble-like monument pays homage to Confederate soldiers and is proudly displayed on the front lawn. The monument is a large column with the sculpture of a Confederate soldier standing on top. He is holding a musket with the butt of the gun touching the ground and his hands gripping the barrel which points towards the sky. Under the soldier it reads: "In honor of our gallant Confederate soldiers." And at the bottom, the words "Lest we forget" are chiseled in the base.

Albert McDonald went on trial for the murder of Cleo Epps Thursday, May 2, 1974. Pugh and McDonald were charged with her murder on November 24, 1971. The trial started a little over three years since her truck was found in the Union Square Shopping Center parking lot at Warehouse Market.

In the state's case, Frank Thurman, the Tulsa County Undersheriff, testified about the car bombing of Judge Fred S. Nelson on August 25, 1970 and that he knew Cleo Epps and talked to her about the explosion three times.

He testified that he took pictures of the box, containing the dynamite that was buried in Epps' yard in her "pond bank." Thurman then identified five pictures he took of the box.

Thurman also escorted Epps to testify before the Tulsa County grand jury in the Nelson bombing. He said the next time he saw Epps again was at the bottom of the septic tank in February of 1971. He testified that two days later he retrieved more dynamite from the box on Epps' property and turned it over to the FBI.

On cross examination from Sellers, Thurman described where Epps was found and that he had known her for around 15 years. He said he knew about her bootlegging endeavors but said he did not know she was a fence for stolen merchandise.

During redirect, Thurman was asked if he knew Cleo Epps was a police informant, and he responded that he and Jack McKenzie both knew.

FALLIS: And can you tell the court and jury as to the information concerning – when you said that she was an informant, what did you have reference to, in that –

SELLERS: (interrupting) Excuse me. Excuse me, your Honor. We object as to hearsay. And it's incompetent, irrelevant and immaterial. And, to allow the witness to go further, it calls for a conversation from the party. Now, the knowledge of the witness or general knowledge of the witness about a common fact, or something –

THE COURT: (interrupting) well, it is established by hearsay to start with.

FALLIS: Yes, sir, your Honor.

SELLERS: Well, no, your Honor. Not as to Mr. McKenzie. And we did attempt to identify the person.

THE COURT: Well, I'm going to overrule your objection and allow his answer.

FALLIS: Would you tell us, in her capacity as an informant for you, sir, who was she telling you about?

THURMAN: Albert

SELLERS: (interrupting) If your Honor –

THURMAN: (interrupting) McDonald.

SELLERS: Please. Just a minute. Just a minute. If your Honor please, that's incompetent, irrelevant and immaterial, and highly improper. May we approach the bench?

THE COURT: Yes, sir.

SELLERS: Comes now counsel for the accused and point out to the court the thrust of examination of the cross examination of this witness was that this woman had been, for years, known as a police informant, for both the police and the FBI, which the witness denied that he had any knowledge of that, himself, and said that he had heard – that there was knowledge, insofar as one other person was concerned, and I dropped it—

THE COURT: (interrupting) Himself, and one other person.

SELLERS: Your Honor, I don't recall that he said.

Sellers went onto argue that Fallis asked an improper question by asking Thurman about what Cleo Epps told him as an informant. He said Fallis knew the improper question would be objected by the defense, making it appear the defense was hiding something. Sellers said he was forced to rise to the objection which is prejudicial conduct.

Sellers asked for a mistrial.

The judge overruled the objection and advised Fallis not to pursue that line of questioning.

Jack McKenzie, an investigator for the district attorney of Creek County, was then called to the stand and testified to his knowledge of the Nelson bombing and his meeting with Epps about the dynamite.

McKenzie said that on the afternoon of August 26, 1970, he was hiding about 150 feet from Epps' residence, and, while he watched, a pickup entered the property.

Thomas Lester Pugh and Albert McDonald were in the truck. They got out, talked with Epps, and then left. He did not hear the conversation.

McKenzie said he later went to Epps' address, got the dynamite out of the ground and gave it to Frank Thurman and an FBI agent. He also said he accompanied Epps to the grand jury hearing.

McKenzie said when he found out Epps was missing in November of 1970, he went to Billie Popovich's house, who is a friend of Epps, and then drove to 51st and Union, finding her pickup truck. The investigator also admitted that Epps was an informant.

John Bough was then called as a witness and testified to living on Epps' property and working for her as a handyman. On November 12, 1970, he was helping Epps paint a barn until around 5:30 p.m. he went home, and Epps eventually joined Bough and his wife for dinner. He said Albert McDonald showed up at about 6 p.m., they talked for five minutes, and then McDonald and Epps left.

John Bough never saw Epps again.

He also testified that Epps occasionally wore nice gold and diamond rings, and that it wasn't uncommon for her to have visitors arriving and departing any hour of the day or night. John Bough also told the jury he saw a 1970 Dodge car at her residence before her disappearance, and McDonald was the driver.

Loda Bough, John Bough's wife, was then called to the stand. She told the jury she knew Epps and McDonald and that she witnessed the two near a hole in the ground where the dynamite was kept. She said McDonald reached down in the hole, grabbed something, and walked away. She said the last time she saw Epps was November 12, 1970 when she left with McDonald.

Before Dr. Fogel, the medical examiner took the stand; the defense offered a stipulation about Epps body and murder.

Sellers said, "We take the position that do not question the fact that this body was found was that of Cleo Epps. We do not question that she was the victim of, uh, murder, involving the – and that the cause of death were the bullet wounds which the doctor describes in his autopsy protocol. We offer into the record the stipulation. And we would waive cross examination of Dr. Fogel on these points."

Fallis refused the stipulation saying, "The state will seek to put on, in this case, matters we feel are relative, concerning his testimony at the scene, and findings – particular findings of the autopsy."

Sellers wanted to prohibit the use of the crime scene and autopsy photographs, as well as the possible gory facts of the murder and autopsy.

Tulsa Police Officer John Uhles was then called as a witness for the state. Uhles is an identification officer and testified to where Epps' body was found and how she was removed from the tank underground. Several photos of the scene were introduced. Sellers objected, but his objection was overruled.

Tulsa Police Identification Sargent Tom Lewallen also testified to the scene, the body, and the removal of the body.

Medical Examiner Dr. Robert Fogel then testified about the autopsy. Fogel, an osteopathic physician and pathologist, performed the autopsy and told the jury her death was the result of two gunshot wounds to the head. He said Epps' death probably occurred in excess of a month before her body was found and probably less than four or five months.

Tommy Gilbert, Epps' nephew, was called to testify about how he "drove, and looked, and walked and searched areas" for his aunt with the help of his father Tom Gilbert Sr. He said he was looking in the area around 6700 and S. Union and found one of Epps' shoes with paint on it. The two men then looked in the cistern and found her body.

Tommy Gilbert denied he found the body as a result of a tip from a third party, despite what was printed in local papers and reported on TV. The paper was quoting Tulsa Police Chief Jack Purdie.

SELLERS: Mr. Gilbert, did you tell the news woman that day at the scene that you found the body as a result of a tip from some person or persons that were not identified?

GILBERT: No, sir.

It was rumored that Tom Gilbert Sr. offered a reward for information leading to the location of Epps' body, and the amount was said to be between $2,400 and $5,000, some even say $10,000 or $25,000.

The state's case concluded on May 9, 1974. Convicted murderer Rubie Charles Jenkins was the last to testify for the prosecution and was brought in from California, where he was serving a sentence for murder. He testified that he met McDonald in the spring of 1970 and the two drove to Oklahoma City in late October of 1970.

During the trip they discussed the grand jury investigation into the car bombing of Judge Fred S. Nelson, and McDonald told Jenkins that he and Epps had dug up some dynamite which had been buried on Epps' property near Sapulpa. He also said the police had searched his car where he placed the dynamite, and they took the floor mat for testing.

During his testimony, Jenkins stated that McDonald suspected Epps was a police informant and had testified before the grand jury due to her relationship with investigator Jack McKenzie and her knowledge of the dynamite. McDonald also implicated Pugh in the bombing.

Two days later, the two men traveled to Oklahoma City, again, and Pugh joined them.

During the car ride, which is roughly two hours, Jenkins said he listened to Pugh and McDonald talk about the Nelson bombing and what Epps could have said to the grand jury. On Halloween, Saturday, October 31, 1970, the three men drove from Tulsa to McAlester and Jenkins said the same topics were discussed at length.

According to Jenkins, Pugh said, "We are going to have to do something to her. If we don't, she is going to send both of us to the penitentiary."

McDonald responded, "That's right."

On Sunday, November 8, 1970, the three men drove from Tulsa to Oklahoma City a third time, and the same topics were discussed.

The following day, Monday, November 9, 1970, the three men met for coffee at the Holiday Inn in West Tulsa, and as they were leaving, Pugh looked at McDonald and said, "Old buddy, we have got something we've got to do in the next few days. If we don't, she is going to send us both to the penitentiary."

"I know that," McDonald replied.

Cleo Epps was killed Thursday, November 12, 1970 in West Tulsa.

On Friday, November 13, 1970, Jenkins said he learned of Epps' death while driving to Idabel, Oklahoma with Pugh and McDonald.

Pugh and McDonald told Jenkins that they got Epps out of the Bough's house and met her at the Union Square Shopping Center. Epps got in the front seat of the car driven by McDonald, and Pugh was in the back. They drove to 71st or 81st and Union and Pugh, using a towel to help prevent blood from getting everywhere, shot Epps in the back of the head, using a .22 caliber pistol. When they reached the 6700 block of Union Avenue, Epps regained consciousness and Pugh shot her again.

Jenkins admitted to living near Epps but said he hadn't seen her since 1969 and said he picked up some stones for his driveway from the area where Epps' body was found.

The state then rested.

The defense presented its case on May 9 and 10, offering testimony that Epps was a well-known bootlegger and fence for stolen property, implying that it could have been anyone in the seedy criminal underworld.

Tom Gilbert Sr. was called a hostile witness for the defense and said he "didn't know" whether he stated that the body had been found due to a tip from an anonymous party.

McDonald's attorney tried to connect Epps with an Arizona insurance fraud case, involving McDonald and a 1970 Dodge Dart. The car had been driven to Oklahoma by Jenkins nephew during the summer of 1970. The car was supposedly seen on Epps' property in early November of 1970 and later found on her brother's property in Wagoner, Oklahoma on November 25, 1970, several days after the police found Epps' truck in the Warehouse Market parking lot.

The Dart had a license tag number of ME-1908 at the time it was found on Tom Gilbert's property, but the tag was issued to a 1968 Dodge four-door sedan owned by David and Harriett Berry of Adair, Oklahoma. The Berry's Dodge was wrecked March 18, 1970 and the insurance company paid the Berrys for it as a total loss. The insurance company then sold the car to Pierce

Winningham, of Tulsa Auto Salvage, located on New Sapulpa Road, not far from where Cleo Epps lived. The car was found in the auto salvage with no license plate affixed to it.

The Dodge Dart, found on Tom Gilbert Sr.'s property, had a safety inspection sticker numbered 811143 that was issued to a 1968 Dodge sedan with an Oklahoma License plate numbered ME-1908. The person that got the safety inspection in Claremore, Oklahoma identified herself as Jeraldine Royce.

The defense tried to establish a rift between Jenkins and Epps over the stolen car and the fence of some stolen jewelry. They claimed Epps kept the car and the jewelry and Jenkins did not get paid.

The defense called several Tulsa Police officers Gus Jones and Lee Nightingale about how no fingerprints were found on the 1970 Dodge.

Judith Brazinsky, a reporter for KTUL Channel 8, an ABC affiliate in Tulsa, testified that Tommy Gilbert Jr. told her that his aunt's body was found as the result of a tip from an informant.

On cross examination, she admitted both Tom and Tommy Gilbert were present during the statement and she could not be certain which had told her of the tip.

Brazinsky then left the witness box.

An anonymous tip would make sense. Murdered witness Tommy Martin Edwards' body was found shot to death in Sand Springs, Oklahoma after an anonymous tip to the Tulsa World, and Dixie Mafia member John

Dillon's lifeless body was found in Chelsea, Oklahoma after an anonymous call to the Tulsa Police Department.

It wouldn't be unheard of that Tom Gilbert Sr. received a tip of Epps' whereabouts but whether he paid the informant is a different story. That has never been substantiated.

It was stipulated by both parties that the 1970 Dodge was found on Gilbert's farm on November 25, 1970 rather than November 26. An FBI report analyzing items removed from the vehicle of McDonald was then entered into evidence and read to the jury. It basically said no connection between McDonald's car and the Nelson bombing could be made.

The September 25, 1970 and March 19, 1971 grand jury reports were also entered into evidence.

McDonald's one-time co-defendant in the case, Thomas Lester Pugh, testified that McDonald was never with Pugh and Jenkins when they went to Oklahoma City, McAlester or Idabel. Pugh said the third man was Burns Trusty Jr.

Pugh also told the jury that he never discussed the Judge Nelson bombing or the Cleo Epps murder to Jenkins at any time. He said Jenkins told him that Jenkins was upset at Epps over a stolen car.

Burns Trusty Jr., a witness for the defense, testified that McDonald told him "that if Cleo Epps doesn't stop fooling around with him, she was going to wind up in a hole in the ground."

Trusty also testified that Jenkins told him, with the aid of his wife, Jenkins killed Epps and pointed out that

Jenkins' house was within one mile of where Epps' body was found. Trusty testified that McDonald was not on any of the trips he took with Pugh.

However, Fallis was able to get Trusty to admit something rather important.

FALLIS: Mr. Trusty, as a matter of fact – as a matter of fact, Mr. Trusty, as of the 23rd day of January 1974, this man, right here, Jack Sellers, represents you, isn't that correct?

TRUSTY: That is on that burglary charge that was reversed.

FALLIS: He represents you. Isn't that correct?

TRUSTY: That is correct. On that charge.

FALLIS: And hasn't he made the statement, in open court, that he is representing you without a fee?

TRUSTY: That's true.

Fallis got Trusty to admit to the jury that Sellers was also representing Trusty in a different case for free, leaving people to wonder if he was being compensated for his testimony.

Everett S. Collins, a former prosecutor and former president of the Oklahoma State Senate, then testified that Tom Gilbert Sr. asked him if he wanted to know who had told them where to find the body of Epps. Collins testified he told Gilbert that he did not care to know.

S.M. "Buddy" Fallis, the prosecuting attorney, was then called to testify about his dealings with Jenkins as a witness for the prosecution.

"I have, since that time, indicated that I would not prosecute Mr. Jenkins for a robbery in Tulsa County, Oklahoma, and I think, the only additional thing that I have indicated would have been that I would make his cooperation known," Fallis said on the stand.

Fallis also testified that Jenkins inquired as to the reward the Oklahoma Bar Association put up for information on the Nelson bombing, and Fallis said it was still available.

Charles Pope, a former attorney of Pugh and McDonald, and the man that ran against judge Fred S. Nelson during the car bombing testified that he never discussed the Nelson bombing with Pugh or McDonald.

Beverly Vincent, a neighbor of the Nelsons, was called to testify that she did not hear anything two nights before the bomb exploded in Nelson's driveway. Jenkins allegedly said to several people that McDonald and Pugh told him that two nights before the bombing they attempted to wire the car and it exploded prematurely. Several other neighbors testified they didn't hear anything either.

The defense then called Tulsa Police Chief Jack Purdie to testify that Jenkins told him in the spring of 1971 that he didn't know anything about the Nelson bombing or the death of Cleo Epps.

The last defense witness was Bill Richardson, a building contractor that, for several weeks, lived in the Western Capri Motel owned by Epps. He said Epps routinely carried large sums of cash on her and had a large quantity of diamond jewelry. He also said Epps and

McDonald were close and never saw any friction between the two. Richardson said he believes Epps would trust McDonald.

The defense rested.

However, the state called rebuttal witnesses, Tom Bunting and William L. Wise.

Bunting, an agent with the Oklahoma State Bureau of Investigations (OSBI), said that he was driving Pugh to testify in court, and Pugh said he could put the murder on McDonald, but he needed McDonald to testify during his trial.

Bunting said Pugh told him, "I'm going to have to talk to my lawyer. I could put this on him, but I have to use him in my trial."

William L. Wise, a rancher in Idabel, testified that three men came to his ranch on Friday, November 13, 1970 and robbed him and his wife. He said there was one unmasked robber and two with masks. McDonald was the unmasked robber, according to Wise.

Both parties then rested.

On Friday, May 10, 1974, the defense's closing arguments started a 2:45 p.m. and ended an hour later. The state's closing argument started at 3:48 p.m. and went until 4:23 p.m. and then the case was given to the jury to deliberate.

The jury retired to the jury room, starting at 4:25 p.m., and they informed the bailiff that they had a verdict at 5:04 p.m. In 39 minutes, the jury returned with a verdict of "guilty," believing that McDonald murdered Cleo Epps on November 12, 1970.

On Friday, June 28, 1974, McDonald was sentenced to life in prison.

After the verdict and sentencing, the appeals and accusations started flying from the defense.

Sellers and McDonald accused the state of not affording McDonald a speedy trial and that defense witnesses were no longer available when the trial started, including his now-ex-wife, Mary Bishop. The accusation is that the prosecution made a deal with Bishop to not testify for the defense in exchange for the dropping of unrelated charges against Bishop. They also claimed that a guilty verdict from a jury in Arizona on an unrelated case was prejudicial against McDonald in this case, and that a riot at the Oklahoma State Penitentiary in McAlester caused more of a delay.

Sellers also claimed McDonald could not get a fair trial due to the coverage of Epps' murder in newspapers, and on television and radio.

They also alleged that McDonald suffered debilitating physical and psychological damage in the 22 months his trial was delayed.

On June 17, 1974, Sellers filed for a continuance for the appeal after a tornado struck Oklahoma on Saturday, June 8, 1974, damaging the Sellers' home in Drumright, Oklahoma.

On July 30, 1976, McDonald's conviction was affirmed by the Oklahoma Court of Criminal Appeals.

The Tulsa Tribune wrote published a tribute to Epps.

Cleo Epps: warm, gentle woman and friend to criminals

By: Windsor Ridenour

CLEO EPPS was not an ordinary woman.

She was a legend who died as she lived: chumming with criminals and skirting the edge of lawlessness.

But there were other sides to Cleo Epps – aspects that never made the headlines or police blotter.

And it was those faces of Cleo Epps that made her a fascinating enigma to those who knew her:

She was, as one friend described, "as tough as nails."

Yet she could be gentle, a warm haven for nieces and nephews and neighborhood children who swarmed her Sapulpa home.

She was a shrewd businesswoman and expert carpenter, building with her own hands houses that she sold for large profits, amassing more than $500,00 in property.

Yet she was a soft touch for panhandlers or persons down on their luck, easily giving without expecting anything in return.

SHE HARBORED criminals, then cried over what they had done.

She sold whiskey illegally, but never drank herself.

It was during the early 1950s she earned the name "Queen of the Bootleggers," a title bestowed by the late

Tribune reporter Nolen Bulloch during his exposes of prohibition liquor runners.

She never liked the title.

And many of her friends never believed she deserved it.

Born on a farm between the tiny Arkansas communities or Blue Mountain and Magazine, she and her two brothers, Sam and Tom, later moved to the rough eastern Oklahoma hills in mid-20s.

An intelligent woman with an innate love of children, she finished a college education during a time when most men and women dropped out of school without finishing the eighth grade.

"She always wanted to teach kids," recalls her brother, Tom. "She stayed with her education until she could."

Her first job was teaching at a little one-room schoolhouse in Wagoner County called Stoney Point – its site now covered by Lake Gibson.

She married then later divorced because she thought her first husband drank too much.

LATER, she moved to Creek County where she continued teaching school.

One of her former students had this to say:

"She was the most warm, helpful lady I ever knew. She'd work with all the kids and give them all the help and love she could.

She was more like a mother than a teacher... she really cared."

She married again and, according to some of her friends, her second husband bought and sold whiskey when it was illegal in Oklahoma.

"She was always strictly against whiskey," said one of her friends.

"But when her husband started selling it, she decided, 'To hell with it,' and got in it all the way.

"That's the way Cleo was – she was either in or out."

For years afterwards, she had a running battle with law enforcement officers, sometimes driving her own truck-loads of whiskey in from Missouri to sell at her stands.

Strangely enough, one of the men who considered her a friend was Jack McKenzie, Creek County investigator and former highway patrolman who many times arrested her.

"I NEVER LIED TO HER, I never mistreated her," says McKenzie. "If I told her something, that's the way it was... If I told her I was going to file on her, I filed on her.

"She respected me for that, and I respected her because even though she did wrong, she was always straight with me."

Most of her whiskey dealings were in wholesale lots, truck-loads of booze she bought and drove into the state.

She once told a friend, "When I invest $10,000 in a load of whiskey, I'll be doing the driving myself."

She apparently was never hijacked during the rough days when competing 'leggers sometimes picked up their booze at gunpoint.

"She never told anybody, if she was hijacked," said one man who knew her well. "I sure wouldn't have been the one who tried it."

Cleo Epps was a soft, feminine-type woman.

Big and strong, she dressed in workman's clothing – usually tattered and smeared with paint from one of her many construction projects around her home or a neighbor's house.

Even in later years, she could "swing a sledgehammer better than any man," recalls a niece.

"She could sit on a plough from sunup to sundown and never even look tired," says McKenzie. "I've seen her out on a place, doing it day after day.

"And she was always helping someone – especially if they had kids.

"If somebody's house would burn down, she'd load up a bunch of furniture and groceries and carry it to them.

"She sure was a kindhearted ol' gal."

IT WAS during the early 50s, when she was running a truck stop in East Tulsa, that a young boy of 11 – apparently a runaway –walked into her place and asked for work.

She fed him, clothed him and took him into her home.

"She treated him like the son she never had," said Tom Gilbert. "She thought the world and all of him."

The youngster, now in his 30s, learned from Mrs. Epps how to be a carpenter and now lives in southeastern Oklahoma.

After prohibition was repealed in 1958, she apparently got out of the whiskey business, although one friend said, "She'd still make a dollar on it, if she could."

She was arrested once, as part of an alleged conspiracy to sell moonshine whiskey in Tulsa and Creek County. She was convicted, but the conviction was later overturned.

Her brother said it was a bum rap.

"She wasn't in on that at all," declared Tom Gilbert, who knew most of her business dealings. "She was trying to help out some guys and they (federal agents) thought she was in on it."

It was that failing – helping lawbreakers – that eventually caused her death.

"I don't believe she wanted to have anything to do with thugs and thieves," Gilbert said. "She didn't want to have that kind of people around her.

"But she had other friends that did," McKenzie agreed.

"HER ASSOCIATES weren't the best in the world. And that's what got her into trouble."

One of those "associates" was Albert McDonald, a big curly-haired man whom, according to one of Mrs. Epps closest friends, Mrs. Epps planned to marry at one time.

An ex-convict, McDonald and Mrs. Epps were close in the mid-60s until her was arrested for carrying a gun during an altercation at a private club as a bouncer.

"She asked me if I thought he'd ever straighten up and I told her I didn't think so... She'd be better off forgetting him," said the friend who asked not to be identified.

McDonald went back to prison and later returned to Creek County, running around a little cocky thug named Tom Lester Pugh.

According to court testimony, McDonald and Pugh knew Mrs. Epps had some dynamite buried on her farm for dynamiting stumps. They asked her for it, and she gave it to them.

But, at the same time, she told McKenzie — concerned, she said, that they were going to hurt someone with the explosive.

BEFORE McKENZIE had time to investigate, the car of Dist. Judge Fred Nelson exploded with Nelson inside. He was critically hurt but survived.

Nelson was opposed for re-election by Tulsa attorney Charles Pope, McDonald's lawyer.

"I talked to her the day after the bombing," McKenzie said. "She cried."

"She said, 'I never dreamed they'd do something like that... what if that little (Nelson) girl had gotten into that car with her daddy.'"

Even with that information, however, law enforcement officers were not able to build a case strong enough to arrest Pugh and McDonald.

Tulsa Dist. Atty S.M. Fallis Jr. decided to call a grand jury, investigating the Nelson bombing.

They needed Mrs. Epps as a witness, and the only person she would talk to was her lawman friend, McKenzie.

"I talked her into talking to Buddy (Fallis)," McKenzie said. "She didn't want to… but she knew it had to be done."

Fallis went to Mrs. Epps home and met, for the first time, the woman he had heard and read about for years.

"SHE WAS VERY polite, very calm, very soft-spoken," Fallis said. "She was very gracious to me."

She agreed to appear before the grand jury, but only if she could do so anonymously.

The last thing she said to Fallis was, "When you're hunting for bear, carry a big stick."

Word leaked out that she had appeared before the grand jury, even though she was hurried in and out of the room, wearing a red wig and disguise.

The rumor reached Pugh and McDonald that she had fingered them for the bombing, according to testimony.

Earlier, the pair had approached her about storing a load of stolen whiskey on her farm – a conspiracy she already had reported to McKenzie.

On November 12, 1970, they apparently called her, asking her to go with them to discuss the whiskey.

For some reason she went.

"She wasn't afraid of anybody," says Gilbert. *"She figured she could hold her own."*

Maybe, as one friend said, she knew she could never run because it would be an admission she had talked.

AS SHE rode in the car with the two, one of them put a bullet in the back of her head.

One witness said before she died, she opened her eyes, looked at Pugh and said, "Lester you killed me. You didn't have to do that."

Her body was dumped in a septic tank.

But even that was not the end of the saga of Cleo Epps.

For more than three months, her body stayed in that septic tank while her family and hundreds of persons looked for her.

Finally, on February 24, 1971, Tom Gilbert and his son Tommy, found her body.

McDonald and Pugh later were arrested and charged with murder. Only McDonald has been convicted in a trial last month at Durant of the Epps slaying.

Cleo Epps was a legend in the annals of Oklahoma crime.

But the persons who knew her best do not remember her as a criminal.

She was an extraordinary woman.

CHAPTER FOURTEEN
A Final Legacy

Life went on, but it wasn't easy, and the death of Cleo Epps didn't stop the fear and stress for the Gilbert family. It only increased until it was evident McDonald and Pugh were never getting out of prison.

During, and after the trial of Albert McDonald, the Gilberts were constantly threatened, and there was a contract out on Tom Gilbert's life. The contract was an open contract and any criminal without a conscience could collect if the hit was carried out.

The Gilberts received threats both day and night, and before the trial in Durant, Tom Gilbert took Cleo Epps' Lincoln Continental to the Ford dealership in Wagoner and borrowed another car to drive back and forth to the trial. He wanted to be able to drive around unnoticed.

One night, the Gilberts got a phone call from an anonymous caller who claimed there was a lot of highway between Wagoner and Durant and a lot of overpasses. The caller wanted the family to know they were sitting ducks for snipers and the overpasses were perfect vantage points for an assassination.

Family members said they were always looking over their shoulders for hit men, and some came right up to the front door and knocked.

Mary Gilbert-Moody, Tom Gilbert's daughter, said that two men came to the house, and Tom knew one of them. The family was home, and the two men were there to kill Tom.

Tom's granddaughter, Shonja Moody, who was just a child at the time, ran between the hitman and her grandfather, giving the would-be gunman pause. One of the men left the house and just started walking down the road, trying to get as far away as possible. The other wannabe gunman said, "I can't do this," turned around, and walked out of the house without firing a shot.

On another occasion, another potential hitman showed up at the house and acted strange. Tom Gilbert, who was already on red alert, watched the man like a hawk. The man really wasn't making much sense and acted like he was there to do a job.

He eventually left without any incident.

One of the scariest moments was when Tom Gilbert's barns were burned down during the trial. It was obviously arson, and there were threats, as well.

At around 11 p.m. Monday, May 6, 1974, two hay barns belonging to Tom Gilbert Sr. were burned to the ground. Tom Sr. was set to testify in the murder trial of his sister, Cleo Epps, and the arson was a message.

At around the same time, the family received threats concerning the safety Tom Sr.'s nine-year old grandson.

The state fire marshal immediately labeled the fires as arson and said they were started by matches. The barns were torched in Wagoner, where Tom Sr. lived, but he was in Durant for the trial. The barns held 3,000 bales of hay and were located one-half mile apart on Tom Sr.'s ranch north of Wagoner on Snug Harbor Road.

The estimated loss, including the structures and the hay, was just under $10,000.

Despite the arson and the threats, Tom Sr. said he would testify willingly at McDonald's trial.

*****

Can a good woman do bad things?

Can a bad woman do good things?

Those are the questions asked about Cleo Epps. Was she a good woman that did bad things, or was she a bad woman that did good things?

Cleo Epps didn't just provide for people, she taught them life skills. She taught neighbors how to frame houses, grow and can their own food, sew clothes, and much more.

Her love of children can never be in dispute. From a very young age, Epps knew she wanted to be a mother, but ovarian cancer took that away from her. She decided teaching children would be the best alternative, and she became a teacher.

However, she wasn't just a mother figure to her students while in the classroom. Epps loved to have kids over to swim in her pond or the swimming pool at the Western Capri Motel. She loved feeding the neighbors during cookouts, showing off her cooking skills while providing exotic meats.

She provided for anyone she could and had a heart the size of Texas.

However, she partnered with some of the most notorious men of that time, and those men would kill without remorse.

Epps hid murderers and criminals in her hotels, allowing some to heal from gunshot wounds. She gave alibis to criminals. She gave dynamite to murders.

She also testified against murders and informed on them to the police when she thought something bad was going to happen.

To be honest, Cleo Epps lived longer than most police informants, and she testified more times than most snitches.

Epps was a complicated and complex woman that waltzed in and out of two completely different worlds. One day she was a bootlegger, hauling illegal liquor to a dry Oklahoma, and, the next day, she was building houses to sell or providing groceries and furniture to a family that lost everything in a fire.

Epps was a good woman that did nice things for people. She didn't do those nice things out of guilt. She did them because she wanted to help people. She wanted to make a difference. She got into the bootlegging business out of a necessity and she remembered what it was like to have nothing and struggle.

Epps was in business with murderers, madams, burglars, robbers, thieves, arsonists, and seedy underworld characters. She was never directly involved with those crimes and always had an answer for why her truck was used in a burglary or why stolen items were found on her property.

Epps never hurt anyone, but she associated with people that did.

Epps was loved by everyone. Judges, criminals, lawyers, inmates, neighbors, students, teachers, and police officials, everyone loved her.

Cleo Epps was an extraordinary woman.

THANK YOU

I want to say "thank you" to my family, first and foremost.

My two children, Gabrielle Joyce, and, Paige McCracken have been my biggest fans since the days they were born. They've always been my source of strength and inspiration through some tough times.

They have been a very integral part of my writing career. I would have never published my first book "Because of the Hate: The Murder of Jerry Bailey" if they had not pushed and even threatened me.

My daughter Gabrielle Joyce is a schoolteacher and a stickler for proper grammar and punctuation. She helped me edit the book and for that I am very grateful.

My son Paige is studying to become a schoolteacher and is also a stickler with grammar and punctuation, but he also helped me in other areas. He helped me put the book together as a whole, working on where chapters should go and asking questions that other readers might have, as well.

Thank you, Gabby and Paige.

To my wife of nearly 30 years, Celeste Lea McCracken, thank you for believing in me and pushing me to create. Thank you for giving me the space to get lost in my writing and the time to travel to do research at libraries and the archives.

And thank you for Gabby and Paige. You have given me the two greatest children a man could ask for.

Thank you to Terry Holbrook for giving me the idea of writing a book about Cleo Epps. Holbrook was a driving force in my first book about Jerry Bailey. He is always available to answer questions about Sapulpa or anything he might have the answers to. Holbrook has been a great friend and a huge support. Thank you, Holbrook.

I can't say thank you enough to my parents. They have supported me for 45 years in everything I have ever decided to do. Whether it was attending every soccer game, football game, basketball game, tennis match, band concert, queen coronation, dance recital, choir concert, awards banquet, etc. John and Karen have been there for their six children, no matter what.

Which brings me to my two brothers Kenton and Kelly. Again, mom will be upset if I don't thank you for something, so here goes. Thank you for making me look so good because I am exponentially more successful than the both of you put together. Maybe if you two tried to be a little more like me you wouldn't be who you are.

I am a published author twice over now and you are still utter disappointments. But, in all seriousness, I love you guys, and the Three Amigos will live forever. We are infamous.

Thank you to my Aunt Cheryl Paige and Glen. You guys have been amazing and were such an amazing help with my first book and have supported me in this endeavor, as well. I can't say thank you enough.

To the family members of Cleo Epps that took the time to tell their stories involving their beloved aunt, thank you.

Thank you to the Tulsa World newspaper, and the Tulsa County Library for allowing me to use their equipment for research. Especially to Tulsa World Executive Editor Susan Ellerbach for putting up with me and guiding my journalism career for several years.

ABOUT THE AUTHOR

Kirk McCracken started his journalism career at the Sapulpa Daily Herald as the sportswriter in 2001. The sports department was in really bad shape, and the newly-hired managing editor, Matthew Broaddus, wanted it to be not only cleaned up, but respected and regarded as the only place for Sapulpa sports information.

Within the first several years, McCracken won several Associated Press awards, including first place in personal columns.

After winning awards, and turning the sports department around, McCracken was hired as managing editor of the Mannford Eagle newspaper in 2008. He won first place awards in news content and feature writing before accepting the job as sports editor of the Sand Springs Leader in 2010.

Three years later, McCracken was named the managing editor of the Sand Springs Leader but left journalism in 2019. In the six years McCracken was at the helm, he, and his staff, have had their fingers on the pulse of the town of Sand Springs, establishing relationships with every organization.

McCracken, and his staff, continued to win awards at the Oklahoma Press Association Better Newspaper Contest.

TULSA WORLD
Thursday, February 25, 1971, p1A, 4A
Thursday, February 25, 1971, p1B

Made in the USA
Middletown, DE
16 August 2020